SpringerBriefs in Cybersecurity

Editor-in-Chief

Sandro Gaycken, Freie Universität Berlin, Berlin, Germany

Series editors

Sylvia Kierkegaard, International Association of IT Lawyers, Copenhagen, Denmark
John Mallery, Massachusetts Institute of Technology, Massachusetts, USA
Steven J. Murdoch, University of Cambridge, Cambridge, UK
Marco Cova, University of Birmingham, Birmingham, UK

T0211824

For further volumes:
http://www.springer.com/series/10634

Cybersecurity is a difficult and complex field. The technical, political and legal questions surrounding it are complicated, often stretching a spectrum of diverse technologies, varying legal bodies, different political ideas and responsibilities. Cybersecurity is intrinsically interdisciplinary, and most activities in one field immediately affect the others. Technologies and techniques, strategies and tactics, motives and ideologies, rules and laws, institutions and industries, power and money—all of these topics have a role to play in cybersecurity, and all of these are tightly interwoven.

The SpringerBriefs in Cybersecurity series is comprised of two types of briefs: topic- and country-specific briefs. Topic-specific briefs strive to provide a comprehensive coverage of the whole range of topics surrounding cybersecurity, combining whenever possible legal, ethical, social, political and technical issues. Authors with diverse backgrounds explain their motivation, their mindset, and their approach to the topic, to illuminate its theoretical foundations, the practical nuts and bolts and its past, present and future. Country-specific briefs cover national perceptions and strategies, with officials and national authorities explaining the background, the leading thoughts and interests behind the official statements, to foster a more informed international dialogue.

Norberto Nuno Gomes de Andrade
Lisha Chen-Wilson · David Argles
Gary Wills · Michele Schiano di Zenise

Electronic Identity

 Springer

Norberto Nuno Gomes de Andrade
European Commission, Joint Research
  Centre (JRC), Institute for Prospective
  Technological Studies (IPTS)
Seville
Spain

Michele Schiano di Zenise
R&D Division
Positech
Procida
Italy

Lisha Chen-Wilson
David Argles
Gary Wills
Department of Electronics and Computer
  Science
University of Southampton
Southampton
UK

ISSN 2193-973X
ISBN 978-1-4471-6448-7
DOI 10.1007/978-1-4471-6449-4
Springer London Heidelberg New York Dordrecht

ISSN 2193-9748   (electronic)
ISBN 978-1-4471-6449-4   (eBook)

Library of Congress Control Number: 2014937691

Printed on acid-free paper

Springer is part of Springer Science+Business Media (www.springer.com)

Foreword

Electronic identities (eIDs) are of vital importance to citizens, governments, and businesses. eID is a core enabler of personal, business, and government processes. The use of eIDs enables a more efficient access to public service and creates trust over the Internet for transaction services.

"Electronic Identity" is a means for people to prove electronically that they are who they say they are and thus gain access to services.[1] The deployment of e-identity will enable governments to offer better government services and reduce administrative burdens. Businesses and consumers use eIDs to enhance business productivity and improve commercial services, such as online bank transactions, signing contracts and procurement, among others.

E-identity is considered as an enabler of the digital economy. The European Union has recognized its importance in invigorating the economy. In its Europe 2020 Strategy, the European Commission drew attention to "the fragmentation that currently blocks the flow of online content and access for consumers and companies"[2] within the envisaged digital single market, and emphasized the need to overcome it. The ultimate aim is to facilitate e-commerce. However, there is still no legal framework for a pan-European system for electronic authentication. The EU aims to overcome the patchwork of different laws, rules, standards, and practices, and to change the legal framework to cross-border transactions. However, it faces national opposition in many member states.

This book is written from a legal and technical perspective.

The legal aspects of electronic identity written by Norberto Andrade examine the core legal and regulatory issues regarding electronic identity (eID) in the European Union. It looks at the main and common objective behind the eID regulatory initiatives and projects developed in the EU: the creation of a pan-European eID legal framework. It elaborates on the obstacles that are hindering the establishment of such scheme and proposes a conceptual framework of principles that could form the basis of a future EU legal framework for the protection and management of digital identities.

---

[1] http://ec.europa.eu/information_society/activities/ict_psp/documents/eid_introduction.pdf

[2] Commission, "Europe 2020: A Strategy for Smart, Sustainable and Inclusive Growth," 19.

Dr. Norberto Nuno Gomes de Andrade, formerly scientific officer at the Information Society Unit of the Institute for Prospective Technological Studies (IPTS), Joint Research Centre (JRC)—European Commission, provides a compelling insight and analysis that are necessary for a broad understanding of the complexities that lurk in the eID regulatory initiatives. This book is stimulating and informative and Dr. Andrade has ensured that all relevant matters have been covered.

Lisha Chen-Wilson, David Argles, Michele Schiano di Zenise, and Gary Wills discuss the user-centric eCertificate system aimed at supporting the eID system. Although the eCertificate and eID are quite similar in concept, their structures and execution environments are different. According to the authors, an eCert file is a collection of selectable support files, individually signed with references embedded in the main content, before it is signed and encrypted with the access control metadata. On the other hand, the ideal eID file will be a collection of selectable text information with an ID image gathered into a single signed file and encrypted together with the access control metadata. The existing eCert protocol that was initially designed for managing eCertificates in a web environment is not able to manage eID in a mobile environment straightaway.

The authors developed a new eCertificate model which they have adjusted to adapt the new eID file structure, so that it can be recognized by the verification process. The eCertificates can be securely distributed and verified independently from the issuing body and satisfy ownership rights, without requiring storage in the verification system. The innovative model thus creates a newly designed centralized verification service for such digitally signed and access controlled distributed eCertificates.

Electronic Identity is a "must read" book which would be useful for researchers, lawyers, policy makers, technologists, and anyone serious about understanding the challenges of a pan-European eID and how it impacts life online and offline.

Sylvia Kierkegaard

Contents

Chapter 1
Legal Aspects

Norberto Nuno Gomes de Andrade

Abstract This chapter examines the core legal and regulatory issues regarding electronic identity (eID) in the European Union. It is structured into five sections. Section 1.2 explains the terminology employed in the field of eID, defining the main concepts and terms of eID and electronic identity management systems (IDMs). Section 1.3 describes the rising socioeconomic relevance of eID, emphasizing its role as key enabler of economic growth. More specifically, this section assesses the importance of eID for citizens, governments, and business. Section 1.4 examines how eID is currently regulated in Europe, focusing on Directive 1999/93/EC on electronic signatures (eSig directive). Within such analysis, the chapter explains the Directive's current shortcomings and the reasons for the unsuccessful uptake of electronic signatures in the EU. Section 1.5 provides a succinct analysis of the revision process of the eSig directive, which is currently in progress. The chapter outlines the main elements and novelties of the recently proposed Regulation on electronic identification and trust services for electronic transactions in the internal market. This section notes how the scope of the existing eSig directive will be considerably expanded, describing the establishment of a mutual recognition of notified electronic identifications schemes and electronic trust services in the EU. Section 1.6 looks at the main and common objective behind eID regulatory initiatives and projects developed in the EU: the creation of a pan-European eID legal framework. In this context, it elaborates on the obstacles that are hindering the establishment of such scheme. As a way to overcome these obstacles and move forward, the chapter proposes a conceptual framework of principles that could form the basis of a future EU legal framework for the protection and management of digital identities: the principles of user-centricity, anonymity, and pseudonimity, as well as the principles of multiple identities, identity portability, unlinkability and negotiation, among others.

The views expressed in this chapter are purely those of the author and may not in any circumstances be regarded as stating an official position of the European Commission.

N. N. G. de Andrade et al., *Electronic Identity*, SpringerBriefs in Cybersecurity, DOI: 10.1007/978-1-4471-6449-4_1, © The Author(s) 2014

Keywords Electronic identity · Identity management systems · European Union · e-Signature directive · Electronic trust services regulation · Pan-European eID legal framework

1.1 Introduction

This chapter provides an overview of the main legal and regulatory aspects regarding electronic identity (eID) in Europe.[1] It is divided into five sections. Section 1.2 defines the most relevant concepts and terms of eID and electronic identity management systems (IDMs), encompassing the terminology recurrently used in the field of eID.

Section 1.3 describes the relevance of eID to the institutions of government, commerce, and citizenship in the information society. This section also touches upon the economic role of eID as a replacement for physical identification for transactions that once required face-to-face verification of a persons' identity, but are now conducted online.

Section 1.4 explains how eID is currently regulated in Europe, focusing on one particular legal instrument: Directive 1999/93/EC on electronic signatures (eSig directive). The chapter then outlines the Directive's current problems and shortcomings.

Section 1.5 examines the revision process of the eSig directive, currently under way. In this context, the chapter describes the main features of the recently proposed Regulation on electronic identification and trust services for electronic transactions in the internal market.[2] This Proposal for a Regulation aims to establish mutual recognition of notified electronic identifications schemes and electronic trust services in order to develop the internal digital market. The proposal thereby expands the legal framework of the existing eSig directive to a comprehensive Identification, Authentication and Signature (IAS) framework.

Section 1.6 takes a step back and elaborates on the main legal obstacles and challenges to the implementation of a pan-European eID scheme. It identifies generic gaps in the current EU legal framework that are hindering the creation of a full-fledged, pan-European eID regime. This section culminates in a conceptual framework of principles that addresses these challenges with the hope of overcoming them. These legal proposals would embed eID-specific considerations into the broader EU regulatory framework surrounding matters of identity, identification and privacy, among other concerns. These proposals are based on the core

---

[1] Specifically, we will focus on issues relevant to the management of human digital identities. Issues surrounding the online identities of objects (namely through RFID tags) and other nonhuman entities fall outside the focus of this chapter, though they are increasingly important.

[2] Proposal for a Regulation on electronic identification and trust services for electronic transactions in the internal market COM (2012) 238.

principles of user-centricity, anonymity, and pseudonimity, as well as the principles of multiple identities, identity portability, unlinkability, and negotiation, among others.

1.2 Definitions and Terminology

1.2.1 What Is Identity Anyway?

Identity—electronic or otherwise—is a complex concept carrying many meanings with subtle, though important differences.[3] At its core lies the concept of sameness (from the Latin, *idem*). This sameness can take many different forms. For example, we can speak of an "American identity" predicated on shared notions of democracy, capitalism, and baseball, among other traits held in common by a majority of Americans. We can likewise express identity mathematically, such that $(8 + 8) = 16 = \sqrt{256}$. Alternatively, a reader can identify with a fictional character by observing similarities between the character and herself. Or we can identify the solution to a problem, which may not be identical to anything in particular (i.e., "the same as"), instead meriting the term identity in the mathematical sense, such that $x =$ our solution, much in the way that we can identify items to put on a shopping list with a simple equation: what we have $+x =$ what we need.

The notion of identity that is most germane to our discussion is that which conveys the unique existence of a single, discrete, individual person, and the various attributes that together demarcate that person as being distinct from other people, or more accurately, serve as proxies for that person's uniqueness. When you pick up the phone and hear your mother's voice on the other end saying "It's me," you can identify her in the sense that you know exactly to whom you are speaking without ambiguity: you can't possibly confuse her with someone who is not the same as her, someone who is not identical to her, someone who is not her.

Of course, as the number of people in a group or society increases, identity gets more complicated. A mother with three boys in the next room cannot summon the middle child simply by calling "Son" into the room. If she calls instead for "David," she identifies David, the middle child's name, as opposed to those whose name is not the same as David. In a classroom with two Davids, the teacher must identify them by first and last name (David Smith vs. David Jones), or by number (David 1 vs. David 2) or some other identifying attribute (Blonde David vs. Ginger David) that differentiates one David from the others. We will discuss identifying attributes in further detail below.

---

[3] The term "identity" is quite difficult to define. James Fearon notes 14 different definitions. See Fearon (1999). On identity as sense of self, see Hildebrandt (2008). For our purposes, we will define identity as "sameness"—recognition that an individual "identified" at one point is the same as the person identified later. On this epistemological meaning of identity, see Davis (2009).

1.2.2 eID 101

Electronic identity is a broad term that captures the information and data that serve as a proxy for a discrete individual person in an electronic context, mostly when stored and transmitted via electronic systems, including but not limited to computer networks. Electronic identities can result from the merger of uniquely electronic attributes and analog characteristics[4]—think of how biometrics blend physical fingerprints with electronic passwords so that a computer can determine that a user "is" who that user claims to be.[5]

Analog identities are determined from an array of attributes like name, height, birthdate, employer, or other features or combinations of features thought to be associated with just one individual. Likewise, electronic identities are built from the various attributes that identify a given person as opposed to somebody who they are not (which together compile his/her identity information). However, in the case of electronic identification, the identifying party is not another person but rather a computer or some other technologically mediated identity management system. Like analog identity, eID is only ID when it is recognized by public and private entities (such as national governments and private companies) as a satisfactory proxy for physical (analog) identity, which is to say that when one party seeks to verify that the person they are transacting with is a specific person and not someone else, they accept this collection of attributes as a suitable identifier such that they can proceed with their dealings.[6]

1.2.3 Terminology

To properly understand the implications of a pan-European eID framework, we must first clarify a somewhat dense array of technical terms.[7] In order to comprehend the notion of *electronic identity*, we also need to understand related and

---

[4] OECD (2009), p. 6.

[5] "Biometrics are measurable biological and behavioural characteristics and can be used for strong online authentication. A number of types of biometrics can be digitised and used for automated recognition. Subject to technical, legal and other considerations, biometrics that might be suitable for IdM use include fingerprinting, facial recognition, voice recognition, finger and palm veins" OECD (2009), p. 7.

[6] A PKI (public key infrastructure) is the most common technical manifestation of this process in eID. PKI uses a pair of matched "keys": a public key used for signing an electronic document, and a private key linked to a certificate that the receiver uses to validate the signature. In this way, PKI can be used to detect if a document has been modified without authorization after it has been sent. In addition, eIDs "may be stored on smart cards or other devices but may also be received from a central authority during an authentication process" Leenes et al. (2008), p. 16.

[7] This section relies upon a glossary of terms provided by various studies and projects, such as the FIDIS project, the MODINIS, PRIMELIFE, STORK, and specific contributions like Pfitzmann and Hansen (2010).

constituent terms and processes like *attributes, credentials, identification, autho-rization*, and *partial identities*.

At the most basic level, we must first distinguish between an *entity* and its *identifying attributes*. We are effectively discussing the difference between a thing itself (e.g., *me*) and the qualities or characteristics that can be used to identify that thing as opposed to something it is not (e.g., my name, which allows people to tell me apart from my twin brother, who otherwise appears the same as me—identi-cal—but in reality is not). Any specific entity (a human being, for instance) has a number of identifying attributes, such as their name, birthdate, address, occupa-tion, nationality, religion, relationships, and physical qualities like hair color or height. The sum of these attributes makes up a person's complete identity. Though it would take a full genetic analysis to conclusively differentiate between two seemingly similar individuals—in the case of monozygotic twins, even this would be insufficient—most of the time we can identify someone by combining attributes until we are satisfied that this combination of attributes is not likely to be shared with another person. At this point, the combined attributes amount to a person's functional identity: they are "the same" as the attributes of that person and therefore serve to identify that exact person, since they are not the same as—that is, not identical to—the combined attributes of any other person.

Just how many attributes are enough to identify an entity? Attributes are themselves complex. Depending on the context or on the attribute in question, attributes can reveal an entity's *full identity*—they can deliver an unequivocal identification—or rather its *partial identity*, a term which refers to an identity characteristic of a given person without revealing her full or entire identity.[8]

Another important term is *identifier*. A unique identifier is "an attribute or a set of attributes of an entity which uniquely identifies the entity within a certain context."[9] In the context of eID, identifiers are digital and fall into two main classes. *Primary digital identifiers* are directly connected to a specific person (e.g., name, address, mobile phone number, password, or electronic signature) whereas *secondary digital identifiers* (cookies, IP addresses, or RFID tag numbers) are not.

These concepts converge in an *identity claim*, a declarative act in which somebody effectively says: "I am me and here are the necessary attributes and identifiers you will need to verify that I am who I say I am." Identity claims are

---

[8] This distinction between full and partial conveys an alternative nuance to Pfitzmann and Hansen's understanding: "A partial identity is a subset of attribute values of a complete identity, where a complete identity is the union of all attribute values of all identities of this person", in ibid., p. 31. For Pfitzmann and Hansen, partial identities may encompass attributes through which a person can be identified. The present definition holds that partial identities cover attributes that do not necessarily identify somebody, whereas those attributes that do identify somebody fall under the purview of full identity. The difference is identifiability: a distinction between information that relates to an identified or identifiable person, and that which does not.

[9] Graux et al. (2009), p. 113. Though numbers (such as national register numbers, VAT numbers, certificate numbers, etc.) are the most common (and, in fact, the default) form of unique identifier, "any sufficiently unique set of attributes pertaining to a specific entity can serve the exact same purpose" ibid., p. 113.

intimately connected with *credentials*. In the offline world, third parties certify claims that an individual is a certain age or lives at a given address and so on. For example, when the state verifies your address and prints it on a driving license, you can make an identity claim against the verified attribute on the credentialed document. Digital identity claims have their own means of verification. "[O]nline certifiers can, by means of cryptographic techniques (security tokens), vouch for certain claims in a secure manner that cannot be tampered with."[10] While paper ID aims to identify physically present individuals, electronic ID allows for remote identification. Conventional ID functions on the basis of personal appearance and paper-based proof of identity (certificates, identity cards, showing one's signature or photograph), while eID is based on more complex processes and mechanisms that take nontraditional identity claims and verify them in nontraditional ways that most often bypass the state.

Identity management systems (IDMs) are the primary vehicle by which electronic identities are created, certified, and verified. The overall objective of IDM systems is to associate information with people, enabling transactions between different parties in an ecosystem of mutual confidence and trust. IDMs are "[s]ystems and processes that manage and control who has access to resources, and what each user is entitled to do with those resources, in compliance with the organization's policies."[11] On the administrator's side, IDMs allow organizations, businesses, companies, and institutions to grant, control, and manage user access to information, applications, and services over a wide range of network services. This access is managed with authentication methods (passwords, digital certificates, hardware, or software tokens) and authorization rights. On the user side, IDMs (should) allow access to all information and tools which a given user has permission to access, as well as the capability to manage their identities as personal data and attributes change over time, ensuring continued access in changing circumstances. IDMs vary widely, each requiring different degrees of identification, access control, and credential management.

In a nutshell, IDMs do two things: they distinguish between users and classes of users (*identification*) and they confirm or deny identity claims (*authentication*). To put it another way, identification functions "link a stream of data with a person,"[12] while authentication functions "[corroborate] the claimed identity of an entity or of a set of its observed attributes."[13] Authentication is about determining who can access what by verifying the authenticity of an identity claim. Just like identity, authentication comes in two flavors: full and partial. Full authentication links a user to a specific person, only granting access once it is satisfied that a specific person, and only *that* person, is attempting to gain access. Full authentication takes place when we try to access bank records or online tax filings that are confidential

---

[10] Leenes et al. (2008), p. 8.

[11] Ibid., p. 1.

[12] Myhr (2008), p. 77.

[13] Graux et al. (2009), p. 113.

to a specific individual or group of specific individuals. By contrast, other authentication functions seek only to verify a partial identity, for example, whether a user is old enough to view certain content, or whether they reside in a region where that content can be accessed, without the need to demonstrate that it is a specific person requesting access as opposed to someone else.[14] In cases of partial authentication, "[the] application determines the entity's status, not his/her identity."[15]

The authentication process requires identity cards, passports, keys, or some other means by which a user can "prove" to a piece of technology that she has the right to access that which she has requested access to. Authentication requires a user to present a *credential* for validation (i.e., "data that is used to authenticate the claimed digital identity or attributes of a person").[16] Digital credentials include electronic signatures, passwords, verified numbers, digital certificates, or biometric templates.[17] Effective authentication involves several actors. To take an example from the European eGovernment context:

> [the] eID process generally comprises five roles, which will be present in most Member States' eID models. First of all, there is an (1) authority that registers the citizen that wants to obtain an eID. This authority is related to the (2) organization that provides an electronic token and the credentials (hence, the eID) that can be used in eGovernment authentication. In addition, the process of authentication comprises the role of (3) an authority that authenticates the token that is used by the citizen. Next to the authenticating party, there is (4) a relying party that depends on this electronic authentication for the purpose of interaction or transaction, e.g. in the eGovernment service. Of course, there is also (5) an entity that claims a particular identity (e.g. the citizen or a delegate).[18]

In a European context, the concept of *interoperability* is of paramount importance. Interoperability is "the ability of a system or a product to work with other systems or products without special effort on the part of the user, covering both the holder of the eID and the counterparty on the receiving end of electronic communication."[19] Electronic identities will have little value for free movement of persons, goods, services, and capital if they are not recognized uniformly by multiple member states—ideally all of them. Anything less than full mutual recognition would undermine the stated objectives of constructing a fully operational single digital market. A pan-European eID would be an "eID issued to persons, mainly natural persons but also legal persons (enterprises, etc.), which can be used in cross-border transactions, and is accepted by all states within the EU."[20] Without technical and legal interoperability, the pan-European eID would fail in

---

[14] Ibid., p. 113. Partial authentication enables people to maintain multiple identities, a practice which will be advocated below.

[15] Ibid., p. 113.

[16] OECD (2007), p. 12.

[17] OECD (2009), p. 6.

[18] Leenes et al. (2009), pp. 25–26.

[19] Myhr (2008), p. 77.

[20] Ibid., p. 77.

its goal of enabling "a citizen from one country to use the authentication system from this country to have access to an application in another country."[21]

1.3 Relevance of eID

Just as the shift to large-scale urban communities undermined confidence in face-to-face identification, bringing about the current norm of state-certified hard-copy credentials, the development of ubiquitous networks of electronic communications, along with the general trends of globalization and increasing human mobility, is forcing us to develop new ways of ascertaining "who is who." Online physical documents are simply unfit for the task. Given the importance of identification to many transactions that are now taking place online, governments and corporations are investing heavily in the eID infrastructure that is needed to support these emerging modes of civic and commercial interaction.[22]

eID also brings various societal and economic benefits to European citizens and the integrated market project as a whole. When citizens can remotely and securely interact and transact with actors and institutions[23] throughout the EU, they can take more complete advantage of the single market, and they can do so with increasing efficiency and convenience. With a functional pan-European eID regime, the single market can become a fully transnational marketplace that can be accessed by any resident, in any member state, at any time, from a number of different devices.

As a result, eID has become a foundational component for EU economic growth. eID not only enables the practical deployment of cross-border services within the EU27, but also facilitates increased entrepreneurship.

It should therefore come as no surprise "that divergent rules with respect to legal recognition of eID and electronic signatures create barriers to the use of electronic communications and electronic commerce, and hinder the free movement of goods and services in the internal market."[24] This is in addition to the privacy and security

---

[21] Leenes et al. (2009), p. 15. Stork cites examples of interoperable eID as those cases " when a citizen of country X can use the electronic identity and authentication scheme of his or her home country for a license application, or when a student from country Y can register for a scholarship in country X with her home authentication scheme, without a need to register herself in country Y." Ibid., p. 16.

[22] Many EU Member States have in the recent times deployed large scale eID projects (such as Germany, see Graux et al. (2009), p. 120.), much of which are presently underway.

[23] European Commission (2010b), p. 11. Such strategic document envisages, moreover, specific and concrete actions in the field of eID. This is the case of Key Action 16, according to which the Commission will "[p]ropose by 2012 a Council and Parliament Decision to ensure mutual recognition of e-identification and e-authentication across the EU based on online 'authentication services' to be offered in all Member States (which may use the most appropriate official citizen documents—issued by the public or the private sector). This Key Action has been pursued through the proposition of a Regulation on electronic identification and trust services for electronic transactions in the internal market COM (2012), p. 238.

problems that arise from a disjointed approach to eID in the EU. When neither service providers nor users can guarantee their trustworthiness in a digital transaction, the trustworthiness of the entire digital marketplace is compromised and a chilling effect takes hold. In a global, digital world, any impediment to digital interaction brings about significant economic and productivity consequences.

Interoperable electronic identities, at the European level, are therefore essential for achieving the free movement of goods, capital, and services that the integrated market project set out to create.[24] Naturally, it follows that eID is also indispensable for the completion of the single digital market, reducing administrative burden throughout Europe and allowing the EU-zone as a whole to increase competitiveness.[26]

Consequently, the EU has acknowledged the need for interoperable eIDs in numerous agendas and strategies,[27] action plans,[28] declarations,[29] communications,[30] studies,[31] and programs.[32] The EU has also financed and supported a vast number of research projects and applied experiments on eID and interoperability (see Table 1.1). In addition to these, many other international networks and research centers in Europe are undertaking important projects in this area, such as the PET-WEB II[33] and the Porvoo Group.[34] Their many differences aside, these research initiatives have jointly contributed to the development of generalized frameworks for trust and privacy-protective identity management systems across Europe.

There is also a compelling legal imperative to develop a pan-European eID framework. Several single market initiatives and legal frameworks presuppose and rely on cross-border interactions between administrations, businesses, and citizens across Europe. It could therefore be argued that in the absence of a functioning pan-European eID framework, it is impossible to fully comply with existing legislation.[35]

---

[24]   Myhr (2008), p. 77.

[25]   Leenes et al. (2009), p. 22.

[26]   Ibid.

[27]   European Commission (2010d).

[28]   European Commission (2010c).

[29]   Such as the Manchester Ministerial Declaration (2005) and the Lisbon Ministerial Declaration (2007).

[30]   Such as the Communication from the European Commission (2010e).

[31]   Namely the following studies: European Commission (2005), European Commission (2007).

[32]   Such as the Stockholm Programme, which lays out the EU frameworks for policing and customs enforcement, rescue services, criminal and civil law cooperation, asylum, migration, and visa policy for the period 2010–2014.

[33]   http://petweb2.projects.nislab.no/index.php/Main_Page

[34]   http://www.vaestorekisterikeskus.fi/vrk/fineid/home.nsf/pages/6F4EF70B48806C41C225708B00 4A2BE5

[35]   This is the case of the Directive on Services in the Internal Market (2006/123/EC), Article 8 of which demonstrates the need for interoperable eID: "[...] all procedures and formalities relating to access to a service activity and to the exercise thereof may be easily completed, at a distance and by electronic means [...]."

Table 1.1 List of research and practical implementation projects devoted to eID and interoperability

STORK	https://www.eid-stork.eu/
	https://www.eid-stork2.eu/
CROBIES	http://ec.europa.eu/information_society/policy/esignature/crobies_study/ index_en.htm
PRIME	https://www.prime-project.eu/
PrimeLife	http://www.primelife.eu/
Modinis IDM	https://www.cosic.esat.kuleuven.be/modinis-idm/twiki/bin/view.cgi/Main/ WebHome
TURBINE	http://www.turbine-project.eu/
BEST	http://www.best-nw.eu/
PICOS	http://www.picos-project.eu/
ABC4Trust	https://abc4trust.eu/
SEMIRAMIS	http://ec.europa.eu/information_society/apps/projects/factsheet/index. cfm?project_ref=250453
FIDIS	http://www.fidis.net/

Despite the various political declarations and initiatives in this area, the plethora of research projects, the proliferation of identity management systems and the wide array of advanced eID technologies, a comprehensive, interoperable, pan-European eID scheme has yet to materialize. Notwithstanding the many outstanding organizational and technical challenges to interoperability, gaps and barriers in the EU legal framework are largely responsible for this critical inaction (as we shall examine in greater depth in Sect. 1.6).

1.4 How Is eID Regulated?

1.4.1 Context: From IDs to eIDs

In small communities, identification is a trivial matter. People recognize each other by face, and interact with a very small group of familiar faces day by day. Increasing urbanization is undermining the face-to-face community all around the world, and with it, traditional identity practices are becoming less workable.

Trusted intermediaries help us overcome identity uncertainty in large communities. The state is foremost among these.[36] By providing an authenticated certificate of identity (credential) that is difficult to forge, the state assumes the burden of thoroughly verifying peoples' identities so that parties who wish to

---

[36] Fearon (1999).

identify them in regular life can do so easily and with confidence.[37] Early versions of state issued-identification allowed approved people to travel, claim benefits,[38] and engage in regulated activities like driving, hunting, or gun ownership.[39]

With the liberalization of the public sphere, private companies are now also engaging in identity intermediation. Banks and credit card companies, for example, issue various credentials that allow individuals to withdraw funds, engage in transactions, and draw credit.[40] Other counterparties (be they public or private) also recognize these privately issued identification credentials in many cases.[41] For instance, many American states accept privately verified credentials as proof of residence for the purpose of voter registration.[42]

As daily life takes on an increasingly digital character, identity intermediaries face intriguing opportunities and challenges. The Internet and other vehicles for cheap communication enable identity-dependent transactions to take place on a global scale. The information age enables cross-border virtual encounters in which physical cues, traits, and state-certified credentials are not suitable identifiers for counterparties who will never meet in person. Even if they could meet in person, many counterparties would have great difficulty distinguishing a legitimately certified foreign credential from a forgery. This reality necessitates novel approaches to authentication and, with them, opportunities for new forms of identity intermediation by electronic identification intermediaries, or eID providers. eID intermediaries must first figure out how to verify and authenticate peoples' identities in a way that is secure, efficient, cheap, and simple.

The European Parliament and the Council introduced Directive 1999/93/EC[43] (the eSig directive) to address the emerging eID marketplace in its infancy, establishing a legal framework for electronic signatures and certification services.[44] The Directive was broadly adopted by the member states, albeit with some variations between them.[45] The Directive, and the EU member state laws that

---

[37]   Davis (2009), p. 220. The process of issuing identification credentials is governed by a variety of laws and regulations that fall outside the scope of our present discussion. For a thorough philosophical analysis of the process of verifying identity with passports, see Davis (2009) pp. 219–220.

[38]   On Social Security Cards, see Davis (2009), pp. 223–224.

[39]   Ibid, p. 222.

[40]   Ibid, pp. 221–22.

[41]   Ibid, p. 222.

[42]   See Voter Identification Requirements, Nat'l Conference of State Legislators (June 27, 2013) http://www.ncsl.org/legislatures-elections/elections/voter-id.aspx for a list of voting ID requirements. For example, many states accept utility bills with the voter's name and address as suitable identification for voter registration (see Alabama, Alaska, and others). Ibid. Arizona voters can identify themselves car insurance cards. Florida accepts credit and debit cards at the polls. Ibid.

[43]   Directive 1999/93/EC of the European Parliament and of the Council of 13 December 1999 on a Community framework for electronic signatures.

[44]   See Directive 1999/93/EC, art. 5.

[45]   Dumortier et al. (2003), pp. 4–8.

followed, moved to facilitate, regulate, and even motivate eID intermediaries to effectively manage identify verification and authentication online. The Directive envisioned that intermediaries would authenticate the identity of individuals upon issuing their credentials.[46] Online credentials were meant to be issued in person upon successful presentation of state-issued credentials like a National ID, passport, driver's license, or photograph (or other biometric means of identification). Thereafter, individuals were issued a technological credential—usually a smartcard.[47] With the smartcard and a password, the individual could: (1) indicate that he or she is the author of a relevant text or the perpetrator of a specific action and (2) demonstrate that a relevant text was not tampered with.[48] Other variations of this method exist, relying on different business methods and modes of identification and technology (including various ways of using biometrics).[49]

1.4.2 The E-Signature Directive in a Nutshell

The eSig directive operates on several dimensions. First, it clarifies the legal standing and validity of electronic signatures technologies[50] for evidentiary and contractual purposes. In other words, it indicates when a digital signature can stand in for a handwritten signature. Next, the Directive sets out a tripartite taxonomy determining the realm of signatures, identification, and authentication. Specifically, the Directive differentiates between *"Electronic Signatures,"* *"Advanced Electronic Signatures,"* and *"Qualified Advanced Electronic Signatures."*[51] The first term refers to the most basic technological authentication measures, which are the least secure of the set, like writing your name on an email.[52] The next two options are more complex, relying on more elaborate schemes for identification and authentication.

The Directive describes "Advanced Electronic Signatures"[53] in Article 2.2 as those which comply with a voluntary regulatory accreditation process and which firms may enter into in order to obtain a quality stamp.[54] These signatures are significantly more valuable than electronic signatures, guaranteeing the integrity of the text, as well as authentication.

---

[46] European Commission (2006).

[47] For a discussion of the high percentage of smartcard usage, see Dumortier et al. (2003).

[48] European Commission (2006), p. 6.

[49] Ibid.

[50] Directive 1999/93/EC, supra note 42, art. 5, at 15.

[51] See Directive 1999/93/EC, pp. 19–20, at 13.

[52] Ibid. art. 2(1), at 14.

[53] Directive 1999/93/EC, art. 2(2), at 14.

[54] Ibid.

In Article 5.1, the Directive defines a "Qualified Signature" as one that meets certain mandatory technological requirements set forth by member states. A "Qualified" signature is based on a qualified certificate and is created by a secure-signature-creation device, which is also called a Certification Authority. The standards required for qualified signatures are the most complex, and thus the juridical value of a qualified signature is stronger than the other types of signatures; qualified signatures enable authentication, integrity, and confidentiality (only the addressee can read the text because the key is difficult to decrypt). Qualified signatures also ensure nonrepudiation, such that the sender will not be able to claim that she did not send the message, and the addressee will not be able to claim that she did not receive it.

The eSig directive also promotes "harmonization."[55] In EU documents, this term usually refers to the act of ensuring that laws governing a specific issue are similar throughout the Union.[56] Yet given the technological context, "harmonization" carries an additional meaning. The drafters were keen to prevent individuals from "losing" their electronic identities when moving from country to country.[57] In other words, they were concerned about people not being able to use their home country issued identity when they moved elsewhere. In this context, harmonization acquires a technological meaning: the need for technological interoperability.

Finally, the eSig directive addresses the liability of service providers in identity intermediation markets.[58] Specifically, Article 6 sets out "qualified" intermediaries' liability for failing to convey the revocation of a signature and similar elements.[59] However, intermediaries can contractually mitigate their legal exposure to some extent.[60] These provisions also allow them to strike down unfair contractual terms.[61]

EU regulators believed that a flourishing market for eID intermediation would fulfill the promise of the digital age by bringing about an international (or at least pan-European) digital marketplace where counterparties could securely identify one another with confidence, just as they would in person.[62] That's not quite how it worked out.[63] While the scope of online actions and transactions has grown exponentially, laws regulating electronic signatures have not substantially contributed to the boom. In effect, the Directive and subsequent laws have not

---

[55] Directive 1999/93/EC, art. 4, at 15.

[56] Commission Report on the Operation of Directive 1999/93/EC, Sect. 3.3.2, at 7.

[57] Directive 1999/93/EC, p. 5, at 12.

[58] Ibid. art. 6, at 15–16.

[59] Ibid.

[60] Ibid. arts. 6(3)–6(4), at 16.

[61] Ibid. art. 6(5), at 16.

[62] Ibid. at 4.

[63] Commission Report, 3.3.2.

generated much interest and traction.[64] EU authorities are aware of this, and have launched several reports examining this failure with a view to remedying it. These reports noted that though member states have enacted relevant laws in accordance with the Directive's general principles, they are mainly applied to eGovernment applications and some limited private banking cases. In response to these reports, authorities created several new structures, namely in the field of public procurement,[65] though these only had a limited impact and could not reverse the lack of commercial uptake.

There are many reasons why the Directive failed to substantially augment online commerce and trust, including the technical complexity of eSignatures and the onset of online business models, especially in the realm of eCommerce, that do not require and thus do not promote the use of digital signatures and other forms of identification like the Directive imagined they would. It takes time, technological understanding, and a good grasp of complex cryptography to fully appreciate the benefits of digital signatures and make regular use of them. Garden variety users may not fully grasp these details, leading them to largely ignore secure intermediation tools.[66] In addition, the Directive was crafted according to a specific vision of the online world, a vision that did not fully anticipate how the eCommerce market would actually develop. As a result, there was little incentive for business to incorporate digital signatures and other forms of advanced identification into their business models.[67] It may also be true that the public is reluctant to spend money on privacy-enhancing initiatives. It is furthermore possible that the Directive did not go far enough to solidify the legal standing of online identity authorization.[68] Not only was the Directive incomplete in that it addressed only one of many types of electronic identification and authentication, it also neglected to offer a legal definition of the concept of identity and how identity can be established in an electronic environment.[69] Moreover, it failed to solve the key question of authentication: "Who is the person with whom I am communicating,

---

[64] Commission Report on the Operation of Directive 1999/93/EC, Sect. 3.3.2, at 7–8; Legal and Market Aspects, Sect. 1.2.1, at 4–8.

[65] Directive 2004/17/EC of the European Parliament and of the Council of 31 March 2004 Coordinating the Procurement Procedures of Entities Operating in the Water, Energy, Transport and Postal Services Sectors, 2004 O.J. (L 134) 1; see also Directive 2004/18/EC of the European Parliament and of the Council of 31 March 2004 on the Coordination of Procedures for the Award of Public Works Contracts, Public Supply Contracts and Public Service Contracts, 2004 O.J. (L 134) 114.

[66] For a similar argument, see Legal and Market Aspects, Sect. 4.3, at 134.

[67] Commission Report on the Operation of Directive 1999/93/EC, Sect. 3.3.2, at 7–8.

[68] One might speculate about other reasons too. For instance, governments' insistence on maintaining backdoor access to many of these systems discouraged users from enrolling. See Froomkin (2011), p. 37.

[69] Graux et al. (2009), p. 118.

and how do I know this for certain?[70]" The fact that member states implemented the Directive in a fragmented, noncoordinated fashion only exacerbated the problem of discrepancies between legal approaches to eID management that prevails in the EU.

1.5 How Will eID Be Regulated? Next Steps

1.5.1 EU Policy and Legislative Initiatives in the Field of eID

Both the EU and members states have recently unleashed a barrage of legislative and policy initiatives aimed at facilitating the acceptance and authentication of eIDs. At the EU level, the revision of the eSig directive and the proposed Electronic Trust Services Regulation are important developments.[71] These legislative initiatives effectively amount to a new Identification, Authentication and Signature (IAS) policy for Europe, which may (hopefully) culminate in a harmonized pan-European eID legal framework.

1.5.2 Revising the Electronic Signatures Directive to Propose an Electronic Trust Services Regulation

The main objective of Directive 1999/93/EC on a "Community framework for electronic signatures" was to promote trust in the digital environment. The goal was to establish a framework for electronic signatures within the European internal market. Nonetheless, and as examined above, the Directive has largely failed in its intended purpose: eSignatures are rarely used in Europe. Moreover, the current legal framework governing eID in Europe is severely disjointed, borrowing haphazardly from the ePrivacy and Data Protection directives, others from the eSig directive, and yet others from national regulatory approaches.[72]

To remedy the situation, the European Commission adopted a Proposal for a Regulation "on electronic identification and trust services for electronic transactions in the internal market" on 4 June 2012.[73] The proposed Electronic Trust

---

[70] Graux et al. (2009), pp. 108–109. As stated in this report: "This is an issue which is not resolved by the Directive, which assumes a prior resolution of the identity question without offering specific guidance".

[71] Proposal for a Regulation on electronic identification and trust services for electronic transactions in the internal market COM (2012) 238.

[72] Andrade (2012b).

[73] The proposal is currently going through the ordinary legislative procedure for its adoption by co-decision of the European Parliament and the Council.

Services Regulation would establish a comprehensive cross-border, cross-sector framework for secure, trustworthy, and easy-to-use electronic transactions throughout the EU. This legislative initiative amounts to a new IAS policy for Europe. The choice to make this a regulation—immediately enforceable in all member states without the need for national transposition—stems from the greater need to reduce fragmentation in this area and thereby provide greater legal certainty and trust within the single market.

The legal objective of this draft Regulation is nothing short of developing and completing the internal market, as per Article 114 of the Treaty on the Functioning of the European Union. It would establish and regulate a series of Electronic Trust Services—eSignatures, electronic seals, time stamping, electronic delivery services, electronic documents admissibility, and website authentication. It will also enable member states to mutually recognize and accept each other's eID credentials, so that each citizen can electronically identify themselves in a variety of contexts in any EU country with a single piece of eID. Member states will be charged with actually issuing eIDs. The main purpose of the Regulation is to enact a common legal baseline for functional eID interoperability between member states, allowing all European residents full cross-border access to online services based in the EU, effectively creating a digital single market.

The proposed identification and authentication scheme will not interfere with member states' own national eID management structures, nor will it impose any mandatory schemes.[74] Rather, the draft Regulation provides an overarching platform that allows states to recognize each other's eID systems, as they currently exist, on a purely voluntary basis.[75] It proposes an EU-wide mutual recognition mechanism through which member states can inform the Commission about their eID systems so they can be recognized by other states, provided they fulfill five foundational conditions set forth in Article 5. Each member state that has notified the Commission of its system specifications must in turn notify all other listed systems.

Though the Regulation dictates that member states must declare the eID systems that they wish other participating states to recognize, it does not mandate that these systems must be controlled by the member state, opening the interesting possibility of state-sanctioned, privately operated eID systems being included in the mutual recognition mechanism. Private companies may take advantage of

---

[74] The draft Regulation clarifies this point: "The Regulation does not oblige Member States to introduce or notify electronic identification schemes." Paragraph 2 of Article 4 clarifies that the mutual recognition and acceptance principle applies only to those Member States that have notified their eID schemes.

[75] Article 5—Mutual recognition and acceptance: "When an electronic identification is required under national legislation or administrative practice to access a service online, an electronic identification mean issued in another Member State which is included in the list published by the Commission pursuant to the procedure referred to in Article 34 shall be recognised and accepted to access this service."

these provisions to access cross-border public services, among other possibilities. However, public-sector eIDs remain the primary focus of the draft Regulation.[76]

1.6 Toward a European eID Regulatory Framework

Many studies have expounded on the numerous and complex challenges of implementing a pan-European eID framework. EU-funded research projects and study reports on eID and eGovernment[77] prepared for the European Commission have primarily focused on the legal obstacles that are currently preventing the emergence of a functional pan-European eID scheme while spending little time on potential legal solutions to these obstacles. This section attempts to fill this gap, and also contributes to research on both these analytical dimensions.

In this section, we review the main barriers[78] to the construction of a pan-European eID framework: the legal blurriness of EU competences as pertains to eID; the divergent—and sometimes conflicting—regulatory approaches different member states are pursuing regarding eID; the disharmonious EU legal taxonomy in this area; and the uncertain legal treatment of identity-related data used in eID transactions between governments, business, and citizens. Later, we present a number of possible solutions to overcome these obstacles with a new generation of legal principles.[79] Many of these principles are inspired by existing technological and organizational eID applications, which emerged even in the absence of an explicit legal framework to govern them.[80] As we shall see later on, many of the new legal principles proposed are derived from technological design principles established in

---

[76] These mainly address eGovernment, eJustice, eHealth, and other public services applications.

[77] Studies and research initiatives led by the Porvoo e-ID Group, Stork, MODINIS, and the IDABC program are exemplary cases, as are studies like those prepared by the eGovernment subgroup of the eEurope Advisory Group. European Commission (2005), p. 6.

[78] We will not delve into the finer details of the legal gaps in European eID regulation law by law or directive by directive. If one were to conduct such an analysis—especially of the Data Protection Directive, the eSignatures Directive, and the Services Directive—it would be helpful to emphasize the shortcomings of the current identifiability model and the need to regulate the processing of certain instances of non-personal data in the data protection framework. For further details, see Andrade (2011). For the eSignature Directive, and further to the ones already examined, one might review the absence of standardized issuing procedures and poor definitions of suitable eID content and verification as barriers to the successful implementation of a pan-European eID scheme. In this sense, see Myhr (2008).

[79] For a more detailed analysis of the legal barriers to the construction of a pan-European eID framework and the proposition of new legal solutions (principles) to attain this framework, see Andrade (2012b)

[80] This is hardly the first call for a balance between technology and law, which is often captured in the term "privacy by design." In this regard, the European Commission noted in 2003 that "...the use of appropriate technological measures is an essential complement to legal means and should be an integral part in any efforts to achieve a sufficient level of privacy protection." In the context of eID, and taking into account the need to achieve a sufficient level of identity

research projects and technical prototypes. We will thus present a set of legal principles with a strong technical heritage. In other words, the legal principles here developed derive from eID technologies that they are meant to govern.

Notwithstanding the critical importance of technology, the main challenge to the realization of a functional, pan-European eID framework is primarily legal. The technologies[81] needed to implement an interoperable eID scheme in all EU member states already exist.[82] The computers can talk to each other but the laws cannot (at least until the present moment). It is the lack of "legal interoperability" that most inhibits the cross-border deployment of eID services. With the facts as they are, the proposed legal framework must not only take into account existing technological practices, but also apply them in the effort to forge a robust set of legal principles,[83] i.e., transpose technological practices into legal principles. The scope of this section is to identify the legal gaps and propose a number of principles that could ideally form the basis of a common EU legal framework for the protection and management of digital identities.

1.6.1 Legal and Technical Barriers

Prior to any discussion of the legal barriers to a fully interoperable pan-European eID framework, we must first bring to light a critical technical barrier to the emergence of such a framework, namely the Internet's intrinsic lack of a proper identity and identification infrastructure. As the authors of the PRIME research project White paper explain:

> The Internet, by design, lacks unified provisions for identifying who communicates with whom; it lacks a well-designed identity infrastructure.[84] Instead, technology designers, enterprises, governments, and individuals have over time developed a bricolage of

---

(Footnote 80 continued)
protection, technology should also contribute to an "identity by design." European Commission (2003).

[81] Microsoft, Shibboleth, Liberty Alliance, Passel, Sxip, and other technology companies and consortia have devoted efforts to building digital identity management systems and tools.

[82] In effect, as the Modinis Interim Report observed: "A commonly heard remark is that for any given technical difficulty in the IDM sector the problem is not the unavailability of technical solutions, but rather an overabundance of possible solutions. Overlooking legal, cultural and socio-political perspectives, from a strictly technical point of view most hurdles to interoperate IDM systems would be fairly easy to overcome," Modinis-IDM-Consortium (2006), p. 7. One may therefore conclude that the most difficult impediments to a pan-European eID are not technical. Rather, they are the result of the different legal approaches and sociopolitical sensitivities of EU member states.

[83] In other words, we are less concerned with the technical facets of interoperable eID systems and more concerned with the legal framework that must be put into place for sustainable, harmonized technical solutions to emerge.

[84] In effect, "[t]he Internet has a ID infrastructure often identifying only the endpoint of a communication: IP addresses. These are often unreliable to identify users." Leenes et al. (2008), p. 1.

isolated, incompatible, partial solutions to meet their needs in communications and transactions. The overall result of these unguided developments is that enterprises and governments cannot easily identify their communication partners at the individual level.[85]

In certain contexts, this is hardly a problem. Advocates of freedom of expression, for example, favor a more anonymous Internet which they feel allows people to more freely express their ideas and opinions without fear of reprisals or other political repercussions. In other contexts, the absence of a built-in Internet identity infrastructure may hinder people, forcing them to "over-identify" themselves and disclose more personal data than would be necessary for comparable face-to-face transactions. Unlike the many face-to-face transactions that can be conducted anonymously—by paying with cash without leaving any identity traces, for example, most online exchanges require purchasers—though seldom vendors—to disclose their identity in some way, usually by having to provide their name, email address—which is often sold to third parties without consent—and physical address. At a more systemic level, the absence of an Internet identity layer also hampers commercial transactions and official government interactions, which rely on the proper identification to proceed.

1.6.1.1 The Diversity of Technical and Legal Approaches to eID, the Proliferation of Identity Management Systems and the Emergence of New Actors

One of the impediments to an interoperable pan-European identity management system is the diversity (and, often, incompatibility) of approaches different EU member states take toward the technical and legal exigencies of securely managing electronic identities. Different states take different stands on a variety of pressing technical matters, including the use of specific Public Key Infrastructures (PKI), the extent to which eID should be integrated into nonelectronic identification methods (such as identity cards and drivers licenses), and the acceptable level of reliance on electronic signatures and two-factor authentication systems.[86]

Likewise, divergent legal approaches to eID abound. While some EU member states—such as Germany and Austria, among others—have developed national eID cards, others—notably the United Kingdom and Ireland—have deliberately eschewed this option. Some countries use national identification numbers for multiple applications, while others prefer to use a unique identification number for each application. In fact some countries, such as Germany, Hungary, and Portugal, have declared the use of one identification number in multiple eID contexts unconstitutional.[87]

---

[85] Ibid., p. 1.

[86] Graux et al. (2009), p. 106, Leenes et al. (2009), p. 25.

[87] That is to say that unique identification numbers should be used only in restricted contexts, not that they cannot be used at all. Discrete sectoral identifiers (namely for tax and social security purposes) are good examples of such restricted use. Sector based identifiers are increasingly popular, partly owing to the aforementioned constitutional restrictions.

Absent a harmonized approach, identity management systems are proliferating throughout the EU,[88] thereby rendering the seemingly commonplace task of identification increasingly more complex. Furthermore, new actors and stakeholders are emerging in the data processing and eID fields. For many, many years, governments held the exclusive prerogative to assign and certify identities and identification documents. Government identification processes were highly centralized, tightly regulated, and stringently bureaucratic. By monopolizing the "identity business," governments were able to more effectively prosecute their other obligations like tax collection, the provision of justice, commercial regulation, policing and security, surveillance, border control, and immigration processing. Today's identity marketplace is far more competitive. It is flexible, decentralized, and less bureaucratic than before, and it is no longer the sole purview of the government. An important shift from government-issued electronic identities to other sources and means of identity attribution and authentication has taken place in recent years, especially online. Social media services, social networking sites, web browsers, and even virtual gaming environments are now issuing eID credentials of one kind or another. While historical identification and authentication processes were about public administration, these emerging forms of non-governmental eID are increasingly social, though the tokens, credentials, and profiles they provide can also be used for secure digital communications and online commercial transactions. In terms of security, integrity, and trust, these new identities are a heterogeneous group, but collectively they constitute an identity universe that operates outside the state's identity spectrum. When it comes to the online world, these non-state eIDs are often more important than their state-issued cousins. They have become the gateways to the digital environment and the various services it contains.

The growing importance of non-state identification and authentication processes is to a large extent linked to the increasing de-anonymization of the Internet. Whereas the Internet was once anonymous—as the *New Yorker* quipped in 1993, "On the Internet, nobody knows you're a dog"—it is now replete with sophisticated architectural models and processes for identifying and authenticating users at every turn. Traditional means of issuing and managing identities find themselves under stiff competition from new, electronic, decentralized, non-state alternatives, delivered by private parties or private–public partnerships. Gone are the days when a single actor served as both identity certifier and service provider. Today, identity providers tend to be separate from service providers. Identity providers act as trusted third parties, authenticating a user's identity to the service provider that requires it. Identity providers also store user account and profile information. Service providers, or "relying parties," accept identity providers' assertions that a user's identity is valid as the basis for partaking in a transaction. This division of

---

[88] There are four primary models of identity management system amid the exploding pantheon of eID systems: "siloed" systems, centralized systems, the federated systems and "user-centric" systems. For a detailed explanation of these forms, see OECD (2009), p. 16–17.

labor allows for the emergence of user-centric identity systems, where "[u]sers are allowed to choose identity providers independently of service providers and do not need to provide personal information to service providers in order to receive services."[89] In this model, users not only select what information to disclose when dealing with service providers, they also select who they disclose it to, with many users employing multiple identity providers simultaneously to avoid storing all their information in one place.[90] We are thus confronted with an increasingly complex scenario, encompassing a wide set of actors—identity holders, identity providers, registration authorities, and authenticating authorities—for which there is no explicit governing legal framework.[91]

A fully functional pan-European eID would need to accept and validate identity claims "verified" by a multiplicity of certificate authorities, while the certificate authorities themselves would "have to relate to many receiving parties in different countries if they want eID holders to be able to make generic use of their eIDs."[92] Given the division of labor between issuing bodies, identity providers and service providers, and their distribution throughout the common market, it is nearly inevitable that the relying party will at some point be situated in a different member state from the one that has assigned the eID, while the service provider may in fact be in a third member state. At present, however, each of these states is likely to implement their eID systems with different technologies and regulate them with different legal frameworks.

Data Protection Directive rules pose further challenges to interoperability. These rules mandate that data subjects (i.e., the identity holders, or claimants) unambiguously consent to the terms and conditions under which their data are stored and can be shared. This becomes a tall order when the data are not provided directly by the claimant, or when data cannot be obtained from a claimant's credentials upon presentation.[93] In these cases, "the service provider (relying party) needs to obtain additional data, such as (certified) attributes and these can be, or even have to be obtained, from other sources than the user." [94]This operation is likely performed in milliseconds via a digital connection between the relying party and the party holding this additional information. Users often cannot consent to this additional query because they may not even know it is taking place, leading to the conclusion that the emerging generations of identity management

---

[89] Ibid., p. 17.

[90] Ibid., p. 17.

[91] Graux et al. (2009), p. 119. Occasionally, one actor can occupy multiple roles. For example, an identity provider can also be an authentication authority, and a registration authority might also be an identity provider.

[92] Myhr (2008), p. 81.

[93] Leenes et al. (2009), p. 32.

[94] Ibid., p. 32.

systems "do not provide adequate safeguards for personal data and give individuals limited control over their personal data."[95]

With such complex, multiparty identification transactions growing routine, it is extremely difficult to hold the right party accountable when something goes wrong. Citizens and consumers are primarily affected by the lack of transparency and accountability inherent to such complex, behind-the-scenes transactions. As a consequence, citizens and consumers will certainly have more difficulties in making informed choices as to which IDMs to use.

1.6.1.2 EU Legal Competences

Any proposal for EU legal intervention and regulation in the field of eID must analyze two important considerations: competence and legal basis.

To understand why member states are adopting a diverse range of legal and regulatory approaches to eID, one needs look no further than the distribution of legislative competences between the EU and its member states. For an EU Institution to legislate on eID, it must first affirm the competence or the legal power to do so. Moreover, any legislation, such as a directive, must have a legal basis[96] and reference must normally be made in the recitals to the concrete enabling power, which generally points to the Treaty on the Functioning of the European Union (TFEU).[97]

TFEU Articles 2–6 set forth three classes of legislative competence: exclusive, shared or complementary, and supporting or supplementary.[98] These seminal competence boundaries pose a significant hurdle to EU-level eID regulation.

---

[95] Leenes et al. (2008).

[96] The basic principle underpinning legal basis was expressed in Case 45/86, Commission v. Council (Generalised Tariff Preferences) where the ECJ expressed the opinion that: "the choice of a legal basis for a measure may not depend simply on an institution's conviction as to the objective pursued but must be based on objective factors which are amenable to judicial review."

[97] In the case of delegated legislation, those references are located in an enabling legislative act.

[98] In more detail, such three categories are the following ones:

- Exclusive competence, according to which only the European Union can legislate and adopt legally binding acts, the Member States being able to do so only if empowered by the European Union or for the implementation of EU acts;
- Shared competence, which constitutes a 'general residual category,' (Craig 2008), as it provides that the European Union shall share competence with Member States where the Treaties confer on it a competence which does not relate to the areas referred in articles 3 and 6 TFEU. Such dispositions deal, respectively, with the category of exclusive competence and with the competence according to which the European Union is restricted to taking action to support, co-ordinate or supplement the action of the Member States;
- Competence to support, co-ordinate or supplement. This category of competence allows the European Union to take action to support, coordinate, or supplement the actions of the Member States, without thereby superseding their competence in these areas, and without entailing harmonisation of Member State law (Article 2 (5) TFEU).

Matters of identity span several competences, often straddling multiple competences simultaneously. The result is a general state of jurisdictional confusion and ambiguity, which is difficult to resolve within the confines of the TFEU competency definitions. For example, eID could be considered a matter of governing the internal market, whereupon shared power is the norm, or it could be regarded as a matter of administrative cooperation, where EU bodies are only permitted a supporting role. Though more a complication than an obstruction, it is also true that eID regulation will likely affect multiple domains within each competence, such as the internal market, consumer protection, and the area of freedom, security, and justice, among others.

The legal basis for EU-level eID regulation is no less contentious than the competency minefield. The Treaty of Lisbon provides at least three legal dispositions (or clusters of them) that could be invoked to justify EU-level eID regulation:

- Art. 77(3) of the Treaty on the Functioning of the European Union (TFEU) which, with reference to Policies on Border Checks, Asylum and Immigration, now allows for the adoption of measures or provisions concerning passports, identity cards or any other such document;
- The Treaty dispositions concerning EU citizenship (Article 9 of the Treaty on European Union—TEU—and Articles 20–25 TFEU), based on which one could argue that the enshrined rights of citizenship require the identification of each individual citizen, presupposing the construction of a European identification system;
- and Art. 16 TFEU: the right to the protection of personal data. Regarding the latter, one could assert that it is in the context of electronic communications and personal data protection, which is—in turn—intimately connected to a rationale of internal market construction, that eID should be legally framed.[99]

1.6.1.3 Control Over Personal Data

The already contentious issue of control over personal data has been exacerbated by the emergence of different technical and legal frameworks in different EU member states for managing and securing the personal data required to sustain a functioning eID regime.

The reuse of personal data is particularly problematic—especially when it occurs beyond the context for which informed consent was originally provided,

---

[99] As a proposal for legal solutions to these questions, see Andrade (2012a). This article argues that the legal basis for the regulation of eID should be found in the combination of Article 16 TFEU (concerning the right to the protection of personal data) with Article 3 TUE, and Articles 26 and 114 TFEU (concerning the establishment and functioning of the Internal Market), which also constitute the area of competence where an eID legal initiative can be pursued.

contravening the provisions of the Data Protection Directive. The Directive is also breached when one party requests more identifying information than is actually required for the purposes of the transaction at hand, going against the principles of fair collection and proportionality.

The variety of technical models for storing and managing identifying data make it difficult for users to effectively control their personal data while also posing serious challenges to any party attempting to regulate these variable practices in a uniform way. Even tracking down where the data are stored can be a tough task, varying widely from IDM to IDM. Silo systems store identity information in distinct service provider accounts. Centralized systems store all user information in a single user account. Federated systems place identity information in distinct accounts stored in distinct locations: one for each service provider. User-centric systems store identity information according to user-selected identity providers. Though the federated and user-centric models offer obvious security advantages, they offer little opportunity for users to safeguard their data after it is has been shared.[100] Federated systems allow users little input into their business-partner agreements, making it almost impossible for users to track their data once it has been distributed to members of the federation, let alone understand the rules that govern this sharing or contribute to them. For their part, user-centric systems pose the risk of consolidation and (over)concentration in the identity provider market, which would then weaken users' control over their own information by undermining their bargaining power relative to providers.

1.6.1.4 Lack of Common Taxonomy

Another legal barrier to the implementation of a pan-European eID regime is the lack of a basic uniform legal terminology.[101] This gap holds true at the EU and national levels alike. The eID Interoperability for PEGS Analysis and Assessment Report interestingly noted that the countries it surveyed provide no legal definition of identity, and that they are equally silent on how identity should be established in electronic interactions.[102] Austria comes closest to a legal definition in its eGovernment Act, defining "unique identity" as the "designation of a specific person by means of one or more features enabling that data subject to be unmistakably distinguished from all other data subjects."[103]

Neither the ambiguity of the regulatory environment nor the total absence of basic legal definitions for key concepts like identity and authentication has stopped

---

[100] OECD (2009), p. 18.

[101] This is the case of the Modinis-IDM-Consortium (2006). Modinis Deliverable: D.3.9 Identity Management Issue Interim Report II1. In addition, the Modinis project developed a specific Terminology Paper, Modinis-IDM-Consortium (2005).

[102] Graux et al. (2009), p 118.

[103] Ibid., p. 118.

IDM systems from coming into effect in these countries. The law may stand still but technology marches ever forward, crafting impromptu law in the process.

An example of "technology implementing law" can be found in Italy, where personal data are encrypted to prevent unauthorized access (i.e., without the user's consent).[104] Thus the technology produces a *de facto* framework for users to maintain control over their personal information in the absence of explicit statutory regulation.

As a result, a number of technology improvements and proposals are filling legislative gaps, effectively enforcing legislative principles and dispositions, while providing certainty and predictability in the regulation of virtual relationships that emulate many aspects of a conventional regulatory regime. This point is well illustrated by the PEGS study, which comments on the legislative gaps in the area of identity authentication and the role of PKI signature technology:

> The main reason for [these legislative gaps] is that, even if the legal framework does not strictly speaking address all relevant issues, the technology/technique behind PKI-based electronic signatures can still offer a large degree of certainty with regard to the entity using an electronic signature (especially when qualified certificates or qualified signatures are used), so that the use of electronic signatures is de facto an adequate tool for authentication, even if the legal basis for it is non-existent.[105]

As such, most eIDMs currently work not on a "legal basis," but on rather on a *de facto* "technical basis." Identity management providers' technological capabilities often dictate the manner in which they store personal data; it is not the case that technical solutions are crafted to comply with statutory requirements. There is thus a need to reintroduce law in this area in a way that assumes that technology will accompany legislation, not displace it. It is exactly in this context, in order to re-articulate the relationship between law and technology, that we will explore the principle of technological assistance below.

1.6.2 Legal Solutions

To this point we have clearly established that Europe lacks a comprehensive, unified legal framework to govern eID. As Myhr put it, "[e]ven though existing laws that regulate a paper-based environment and physical ID-cards to a large extent can also be applied to electronic communication and the use of eIDs, an appropriate regulation regarding eID on a European level is lacking."[106] In fact the reality is more acutely problematic. The direct application of current EU Directives to eID does not adequately address the many data protection and identity management issues unique to eID. As we mentioned previously, the unsystematic

---

[104] Ibid., p. 128.

[105] Ibid., p. 119.

[106] Myhr (2008), p. 77.

agglomeration of rules that stands in for a comprehensive eID legal framework are deeply fractured and disjointed, borrowing piecemeal from the ePrivacy Directive, the eSignatures Directive, member state regulations, and the technical realities of the eID industry that emerged in the absence of explicit regulation.

Europe needs a legal framework that "[e]nsures interoperability for trustworthy authentication across service domains of Member State public authorities, business and citizens,"[107] allowing for "EU-wide trustworthy service provisioning in domains such as e-government, e-health, e-commerce, finances and social networks, and hence should support the provisioning of multiple identity instances from government-accredited to commercially accepted, ranging from strong identification to anonymity."[108]

To connect national and regional IDM systems into an interoperable EU-level eID regime, we must overcome far more than simple technical obstacles of network compatibility. Legal interoperability is desperately wanting. By establishing a few common legal principles, the interoperability impasse might finally be cleared.

Since the 1980s, the core principles of personal data protection have been set forth by a series of international arrangements and agreements. The Organization for Economic Cooperation and Development (OECD) adopted the Guidelines on the Protection of Privacy and Transborder Flows of Personal Data in 1980, and the Council of Europe followed in 1981 with the Convention for the Protection of Individuals with regard to Automatic Processing of Personal Data. In the 1990s, the EU's Data Protection Directive (DPD) advanced this effort with a list of principles stipulating the manner in which personal data ought to be handled. These initiatives have yielded an extensive list of principles regarding data collection, storage, and processing, including *collection limitation, data quality, purpose specification, use limitation, security safeguards, openness, individual participation*, and *accountability*.[109]

---

[107] van Rooy and Bus (2010), p. 403.

[108] Ibid., p. 403.

[109] The basic principles are listed in Article 6 of the Data Protection Directive (DPD), and include the requirements that personal data must be:

(a) processed fairly and lawfully;

(b) collected for specified, explicit, and legitimate purposes and not further processed in a way incompatible with those purposes. Further processing of data for historical, statistical, or scientific purposes shall not be considered as incompatible provided that Member States provide appropriate safeguards;

(c) adequate, relevant and not excessive in relation to the purposes for which they are collected and/or further processed;

(d) accurate and, where necessary, kept up to date; every reasonable step must be taken to ensure that data which are inaccurate or incomplete, having regard to the purposes for which they were collected or for which they are further processed, are erased or rectified;

(e) kept in a form which permits identification of data subjects for no longer than is necessary for the purposes for which the data were collected or for which they are further processed. Member States shall lay down appropriate safeguards for personal data stored for longer periods for historical, statistical or scientific use.

Were these existing principles buttressed by some additions, they would, together with the current EU legal framework, bridge many gaps in EU law, and pave the way for a uniform, comprehensive, pan-European eID regulatory regime.

The foundational work that has already been done in this area[110] provides us with ample material with which to craft a coherent conceptual framework for eID governance in Europe. Such a framework groups the most salient elements of these foundational materials into clusters of principles and rules that complement existing data protection principles and address their eID-specific gaps. We can also formulate legal principles by observing the functional dynamics of identity management systems as they currently operate to derive juridical lessons from their construction and to anticipate solutions to potential problems that may arise in future. As Dumortier observes, "[t]he field of privacy and identity management will be an important laboratory where we can experiment how the law will function in our future global information society."[111]

User-centricity is the overarching legal principle we shall discuss. Within the principle of user-centricity resides a set of key principles that ensure *individual autonomy* in the management of one's eID. One of these sets of principles underlines the importance of users being able to employ multiple identities, use pseudonyms, or otherwise pursue anonymity online (*principle of multiple identities, pseudonymity and anonymity*). Another descendant cluster of the principle of user-centricity is formed of a series of technical, procedural principles that enable users to maintain a clear separation between their various identities (*unlinkability*) and ensure full control of their personal information (*negotiation, portability,* and *authentication source*). *Technological assistance,* within the procedural principles group, underlines the important symbiosis of technological development and the legal structures that regulate it (see Fig. 1.1) .

These principles alone do not constitute a fully functional eID framework, but in conjunction with concrete rules,[112] policies, and technological infrastructure developments, they would amount to such a comprehensive framework.

(Footnote 109 continued)

A part from these basic principles, Article 7 of the DPD delineates the conditions under which personal data may be processed, amidst which we stress the requisite that "the data subject has unambiguously given his consent".

[110] Such as the EU/EC programmes, commissioned studies, action plans, agendas and research projects promoted in the eID area and mentioned in Sect. 1.3.

[111] Dumortier (2003), p. 69.

[112] In terms of concrete proposals for the achievement of a pan-European electronic ID scheme, Thomas Myhr presents two concrete action proposals that the European Commission could take into consideration in order to achieve cross-border interoperability: (i) setting up requirements for Validation Authorities and self-declaratory schemes and (ii) setting up a quality classificatory system, where different national security levels can be mapped against neutral requirements adopted by the European Commission. See Myhr (2008).

Fig. 1.1 eID legal
framework principles

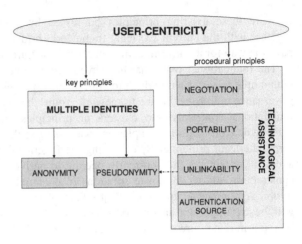

1.6.2.1 Principle of User-Centricity

The principle of user-centricity sets out to "create the knowledge society by empowering the individual,"[113] giving individuals full control over their identity information. A user-centric legal framework places the individual to be identified at the core of the IDM system, while continuing to respect broader social and commercial interests.

Many identity management systems are already user-centric in the technical sense of the term. Unlike federated IDMs, user-centric systems are non-hierarchical associations of multiple service providers and identity providers. Identity providers participate as trusted third parties charged with user authentication and account and profile storage responsibilities. Service providers, also called "relying parties," receive authenticated identity claims from identity providers and accept this authenticated claim as the basis for providing the requesting party with services or access to secured information. This arrangement empowers users to select identity providers independently of service providers and also obviates the need to disclose sensitive information to service providers as a condition of transacting with them.[114] Users can decide what information they choose to disclose to service providers—within certain limits, depending on the type of transaction[115] —while also having the option to employ more than one identity provider should users find themselves concerned about having all their information stored in one place.[116] By endowing data subjects with effective control over their personal data, user-centricity reinforces the existing principles of data protection—namely specification,

---

[113] European Council (2010), p. 43.

[114] OECD (2009), p. 17.

[115] Ibid., p. 17.

[116] Ibid., p. 17.

fair collection and accuracy, minimization, adequacy, and proportionality—while also enabling the "right to be forgotten."[117]

Like all well-calibrated legal principles, user-centricity must balance users' data management interests with the interests of other affected parties like the government and corporate actors. For public safety reasons or other similar considerations, governments may have legitimate grounds to access and share citizens' personal data without their expressed consent.[118] Maintaining this balance of interests between individual citizens, the private sector, and the government is among the greatest challenges involved in crafting a coherent, functioning legal framework for governing eID. The same could be said of the legitimate interest of private sector actors, which often conflict with the legitimate interest of citizens or the state. Any effective framework must acknowledge these tensions and develop a workable mechanism for mediating between competing claims and reconciling differences.

1.6.2.2 Principle of Multiple Identities

Jones and Martin are apt to note that "[t]he issue of what we consider to be the identity of a person has become increasingly complex as we have made ever greater use of the facilities and services that have been made available by developing technologies and the Internet. In the past, people normally had one identity, while in the current environment it is acceptable to maintain separate 'identities' for different aspects of our online interactions."[119]

People today can and do maintain multiple partial identities, leaving them free to choose which they prefer to deploy in a given context. As Nabeth notes, these identities are continually evolving, even in the offline world:

> …as individuals take on many different roles in the course of their life, different set of characteristics, corresponding to these different roles, are used to represent their identity. Each of these 'partial identities' includes both inherited 'timeless' characteristics (such as nationality, gender, etc.) and characteristics that they have acquired during their life (such as diplomas, competences, etc.), or that they have been assigned or issued to fulfill this role (such as a position, some sort of authority, etc.).[120]

---

[117] That is, "the right of individuals to have their data no longer processed and deleted when they are no longer needed for legitimate purposes", European Commission (2010a), p 8.

[118] Mary Rundle lists the following examples of legitimate governance reasons for accessing and sharing citizens' personal data: "For example, in fighting cybercrime, governments want authority to require Internet service providers to hand over subscriber information, among other data. To facilitate travel, governments have agreed to certain standards for a global system of electronic identity information. For taxation of international e-commerce, OECD members are seeking reliable ways to identify taxpayers. To counter the financing of terrorists or other criminals, governments seek to ensure that information on originators of wire transfer is available" Rundle (2006).

[119] Jones and Martin (2010), p. 1.

[120] Nabeth (2009), p. 38.

In addition to the collection of partial identities that a person amasses in the physical world, that person will likely maintain a host of partial identities to use online. They may have accounts on various social networking sites (or within the same one) registered under different usernames, or they may present different avatars in online games and virtual realities. An individual may identify herself by a pseudonym on an online message board while presenting her civil identity for business transactions or to access e-government services. Individuals disclose different identifying attributes to different counterparties, such that when these counterparties attempt to discern someone's "complete" identity by aggregating the partial attributes they have on file, they will invariably arrive at conclusions that are not necessarily identical.

In face-to-face interactions it takes a great deal of guile and disguise to avoid disclosing certain identity attributes like height, gender, race, or (approximate) age. Selective disclosure is much easier in digital interactions. It is even possible to create new attributes and features that do not exist offline, bringing about a new, alternative identity without the need for radical actions like forging of state documents.

The ease with which people can assume multiple identities online can be problematic and it is not without risk. People tend to accumulate many "digital personae," which can be tough to keep track of. Thus, the privacy of that "multifaceted" person will be vulnerable to compromise when a person has forgotten about a certain segment of their online activities or when they fail to account for the full spectrum of their online identities when implementing security measures like password changes. And once data pertaining to one partial identity are shared with third parties, it is almost impossible to take them back. As others have noted, "[u]nlike goods, data cannot be reclaimed without the possibility that a copy is left behind in several possible places."[121] The principle of multiple identities must therefore ensure that identity management systems provide users with the tools required to effectively manage their multiple identities and reclaim data, even after it is shared with a third party.[122] In this way, the principle of multiple identities reinforces the extant principle of data minimization. Enhanced user control over data disclosure, covering any and all digital personae they elect to maintain, will result in decreased data disclosure.

The principle of multiple identities also addresses the risks inherent to using a single digital identity in multiple online contexts. As Poullet observes, "[i]t is clear that, most often, the same identification method or access key is used in different databases with [the] result that our identity can be cross-referenced more easily."[123] Practices like storing national registration numbers in all governmental

---

[121] Leenes et al. (2008), p. 9.

[122] The PRIME research project, in its technical proposals and prototypes for privacy-identity management tools, envisaged three central means of controlling multiple partial identities: tracking one's data trail, support for rights enforcement and policy enforcement. See ibid., p. 9.

[123] Poullet (2010), p. 11.

databases "increases the possibility of cross-referencing the information and thus, enhances the power of the state (...) vis-à-vis the citizen."[124] To guard against this imbalance, the principle of multiple identities must inhibit identity cross-referencing to restore the traditional balance of power between state and citizen, as it existed before the advent of the Internet.

At the technological level, the principle of multiple identities is mature and well developed. For example, The PRIME project proposed a PRIME Console as tool for enhanced and secure online identity management. Among its various features, the PRIME Console would allow users to create partial identities (pseudonyms) and to associate personal data with these identities.[125] The TURBINE project offers another technical implementation of the principle of multiple identities—as well as the principle of unlinkability, as we shall see below.[126] This research program set out to enable people "to create different 'pseudo-identities' for different applications with the same fingerprint, whilst ensuring that these different identities (and hence the related personal data) cannot be linked to each other."[127]

1.6.2.3 Principle of Anonymity and Pseudonymity

As a general principle, identity systems should enable anonymity and pseudonymity. These systems should also provide detailed rules regulating the use of anonymous and pseudonymous data. eID legal frameworks should explicitly regulate the cases in which people have the right to conceal their identity data (*anonymisation*) or to present a different identity (*pseudonymisation*), and the circumstances under which these masks can reasonably be lifted. IDM systems should allow for anonymity or pseudonymization by default for most commercial transactions. Commercial service providers only require a limited range of clients' identity attributes to confidently transact with them. Think of it like online cash: customers can handle the vast majority of their transactions anonymously should they choose, without compromising the interests of the vendor in any way.

Anonymity and pseudonymity are intrinsically linked to the existing data minimization principle. A workable legal framework would need to establish clear exceptions for specific interactions where some greater interest would be compromised by an obscured identity. These exceptions might include public administration interactions like tax collection, voting, or benefits administration, in which there is no suitable replacement for an individual's singular, individual, civic identity.

---

[124] Ibid., p. 11.

[125] Leenes et al. (2008), p. 5.

[126] The TURBINE project aims to develop innovative digital identity solutions. They employ electronic fingerprint authentication to ensure secure, automatic user identification and apply advanced cryptography technologies to reliably protect biometric data. For further information, see http://www.turbine-project.eu/

[127] http://www.turbine-project.eu/

Exceptions aside, the principles of anonymity and pseudonymity acknowledge the simple commercial fact that for most transactions, a limited selection of identity attributes is enough to satisfy the privacy and verification needs of both vendors and customers. In this area, technology is a (giant) step ahead of the law, with many identity management tools already offering anonymity and pseudonymity by default, where appropriate, even in the absence of an explicit legal imperative to do so.[128] For example, the PRIME Console automatically creates unique pseudonyms for each user transaction, making it more difficult for potential priers to discern sensitive information about the "real" person by following a pseudonym trail online.[129]

Naturally, the principles of anonymity and pseudonymity are not absolute—they are limited and those limits ought to be explicitly defined in the eID legal framework. The principles of anonymity and pseudonymity should not preclude legally justifiable mechanisms for unveiling civil identities in specific instances such as breach of contract or the suspected perpetration of a criminal act, among other potential reasons.[130] Any legal framework that adopts the principles of anonymity and pseudonymity should circumscribe the cases in which anonymous and pseudonymous identities are permissible, and those in which they are not.

1.6.2.4 Principle of Unlinkability

Linkability is a complex and contested issue. Online vendors tend to exchange information regarding users' habits, tastes, and preferences to tailor products and services to specific users. They do this for their own interest—to sell more products—but a strong argument could also be made that this practice benefits users by making it easier for them to find what they want, thereby rendering the marketplace more efficient from the consumer standpoint. However, users also maintain a legitimate interest in choosing to disclose their identities to some service providers while withholding it from others.

As we have seen, the principles of multiple identities and pseudonymity allow users the freedom to choose which identity attributes they disclose at any given time. However, it is not enough to be able to create and maintain multiple identities and pseudonyms, it is also necessary to keep them separate. The principle of

---

[128] "... anonymous, or pseudonymous interactions are the default within PRIME ... PRIME supports different forms of pseudonymous with different characteristics with respect to linkability ." Leenes et al. (2008), p. 8.

[129] As remarked in the PRIME project White paper: "If I know your name, I can try to get data about you through all sort of channels, which is much more difficult if I only know your transaction pseudonym ghT55897" ibid., p. 8.

[130] Mechanisms exist to reveal the identity of users when warranted and under strict conditions. As a concrete proposal, it is suggested that "[o]ne of these conditions would be the use of a trusted third party that is contractually bound to reveal the civil identity of the user under certain circumstances." ibid., p. 11.

unlinkability prevents counterparties from accessing information from different sources that they could potentially use to reconstruct the identity of a person who chooses to disclose only a limited selection of attributes with the goal of transacting anonymously. Unlinkability is particularly relevant to "pseudonymisation." By keeping pseudonyms separate from one another, they cannot be used to deduce full or exact identities, effectively preventing *de-pseudonymization* and *de-anonymization*.[131]

Technology designers are aware of the possible risks of unintended attribute linkage and they have taken measures to mitigate these risks. For example, the PRIME project envisioned the creation of multiple private credentials from a single master certificate. Credentials, which could correspond to different pseudonyms belonging to the same person, would be unlinkable to each other and to the master certificate from which they were derived. Another technical application of unlinkability can be found in the case of the Austrian sourcePin, which works as an "obfuscated identifier."[132] This number is never used to directly authenticate the user in eGovernment applications. Instead, it is used to generate sector-specific personal identification numbers (PINS), which are then passed on to counterparties. PINS are created with cryptographic one-way functions to keep them unlinkable, so that "the citizen is uniquely identified in one sector, but identifiers in different sectors cannot be lawfully cross-related."[133] In this way, IDM systems use unlinkability to mitigate the risk of unintended cross-referencing between pseudonyms and multiple identity attributes used by the same person online.

Touching upon a number of proposals advanced here, Dumortier argues that:

> Future solutions will have to give data subjects maximum possibilities to control and steer the use of their personal data. They should be flexible enough to offer possibilities for the data subject to reveal only the identification data that are necessary for particular circumstances. Anonymous use of network services should be guaranteed where it is reasonably admissible. If unconditional anonymity—whereby the identity of the user is irreversibly lost—is not feasible, privacy-protecting schemes for conditional anonymity have to be established. Consequently the use of multiple "virtual identities" will have to be regulated.[134]

---

[131] De-anonymisation of data is becoming a recurrent phenomenon, posing new risks to privacy. In this respect, see Ohm (2009).

[132] Graux et al. (2009), p. 115.

[133] In also observing the principle of unlinkability, the same study points out that the Czech republic plans to implement a similar system to the Austrian one, "based on the introduction of a 'basic personal identifier', which will be used to derive a set of personal identifiers for specific contexts, so that each individual will be identified by a different identifier in each context" ibid., p. 115., avoiding thus for different eIDs to be cross-related and linked.

[134] Dumortier (2003) p. 69.

1.6.2.5 Principle of Negotiation

The principle of *negotiation* would provide users with the flexibility to arbitrate the terms and conditions under which they disclose identity information. Negotiation allows users to contribute to the definition of the manner in which they can access, correct, and delete personal data after they are disclosed. Without negotiation, user consent is fairly meaningless. Without the right to negotiate, consumers must either comply with vendor identification demands—no matter how proportional they are relative to the needs of the transaction at hand—or choose exclusion. In such an arrangement, the bargaining positions of customers and vendors are poorly balanced.[135]

Negotiation would provide a valuable counterbalance to the prevalent "take it or leave it" approach that currently undermines the user consent requirement. Negotiation would enhance users' ability to control how their personal identity data are processed and managed. Negotiation is derived from user-centricity and aims to reinforce (and surpass) mere consent as the benchmark for lawfully processing personal identity data. The principle of negotiation thus serves to help the coming generation of identity management systems empower users to arbitrate the conditions under which their identities are managed, shared, and protected. The PRIME project has already experimented with negotiation:

> PRIME replaces the "take it or leave it" approach to privacy policies by a system of policy negotiation. Both parties can express different kinds of policies relating to authorizations, data handling, and preferences. The user is assisted by the PRIME Console that helps in setting personal preferences and requirements, in converting preferences from machine readable form to human readable form and vice versa, and in automatically negotiating the user's preferences with the other party.[136]

1.6.2.6 Principle of Portability

The principal of *portability* owes its *raison d'être* less to privacy concerns than to a strict and specific identity rationale. Privacy in the classical sense is a right to *not* be identified or to keep private matters from public view, preventing disclosed information from reaching the public sphere. Identity, on the other hand, involves the deliberate transmission of information to the public sphere. When we choose to convey our information to the public, we have a strong interest in ensuring that it is conveyed accurately and correctly. To properly identify yourself in a variety of contexts, you must be able to carry your identity with you. In other words, your identity must be portable. Portability prohibits identity management providers from preventing users from taking their constructed identities elsewhere, since such a move would likely inhibit people from accurately and positively identifying themselves in all contexts.

---

[135] Leenes et al. (2008), p. 3.

[136] Ibid., p. 7.

The principle of portability holds that digital identities and the reputations associated with them must be easily transferable between service or identity providers. Portability is especially germane to electronic reputations. Reputations are a burgeoning aspect of the online world. Many online communities allow users to be evaluated or rated by their peers for certain skills or expertise that may prove valuable. Credit scores, endorsements, recommendations, and skills assessments can translate into job prospects, advantageous interest rates, and many other prospective benefits. But despite the rapid emergence of these peer reputation communities, it is difficult to transfer reputations between communities. In the rare event that a reputation is portable, it is seldom possible to transfer reputations anonymously. As the PRIME project observed, "[t]ransferring reputations from one context to the next, without linkability of the underlying partial identities, is a feature that will prove valuable in online interactions."[137] Technology in this instance once again preempts the law. PRIME has proposed a technical system for mediating reputation transfer with anonymous credentials, offering an interesting intermingling of the principles of portability and anonymity.

Portability is particularly innovative because the current data protection framework is skewed toward (negative) privacy considerations as opposed to (positive) identity considerations.[138] For example, the current right to access, correct, and delete private information is driven primarily by privacy concerns, with little concern for people's ability to move their information between services.

1.6.2.7 The Authentication Source Principle

The *authentication source principle* holds that "for each given attribute (piece of identity data), one and only one source is considered to be authentic, i.e., correct."[139] In other words, the authentication source principle ensures that one and only one authentic source should be correlated with a specific identity attribute, rendering all other sources for that attribute redundant, and therefore dispensable. This principle is derived from member states' statutory treatment of national identity registers and eGovernment services.

The authentication source principle "is relevant from a cross border interoperability perspective, because a consistent application of the authentic source principle means that a single correct source exists for each bit of information, which can facilitate the access and exchange of this information."[140]

---

[137] Ibid., p. 10.

[138] In this sense, see Andrade (2011a, b).

[139] Graux et al. (2009), p. 112.

[140] Ibid., p. 81. For more information on which countries surveyed in the PEGS study subscribed to an authentication source principle and to what extent this principle has impacted their identity management policies, see ibid., pp. 81–84.

Knowing that each of their identity attributes can be verified from one source and one source only, the task of managing identity attributes becomes far more streamlined for users. They will be spared the need to repeatedly produce the same piece of information and when their identity information changes, they will know that it must only be updated once, ensuring they can accurately represent themselves at all times, further buttressing the principle of data accuracy.[141]

1.6.2.8 Principle of Technological Assistance

The law has its limits. For example, the majority of EU member states have no legal recourse to permit their national identity numbers to be accepted beyond their borders, just as they lack the legal mechanism to disseminate unique identifiers for use across the EU. The pan-European eID project can only be realized if all EU citizens can use their eIDs to access services in all member states, meaning that all member states must have some way of identifying all citizens. If legal avenues toward this goal are practically impassable, technology might present a viable alternative route. Besides, interoperability on this scale would require significant technical developments that cannot simply be legislated into being. For example, the issue of transferable identifiers might be resolved by a "one-way transformation function that unequivocally transforms a foreign ID number into one that may be locally stored."[142] This example brings to light the limitations of the law and the need for accompanying technologies that translate statutory principles into daily reality. Technology can pick up where the law can no longer proceed, while also providing practical opportunities to enforce legislative principles. The principle of technological assistance may, for example, lead authorities to impose technical standards on terminal equipment manufacturers in order to ensure compliance with digital identities protection and management regulations. It may also lead to the construction of new and fully fledged rights.[143]

Technological assistance is already a reality. For example, Art. 29 Data Protection Working Party explicitly recommends that software and hardware products should be equipped to comply with EU data protection rules.[144] Privacy Enhancing Technologies (PETs) and the "Privacy by Design" approach are further examples of technical assistance to legal measures, as is the emerging trend of Data

---

[141] Ibid., p. 112.

[142] Leenes et al. (2009), p. 32.

[143] In this context, see Poullet's construction of a "new privacy right: the right to a privacy compliant terminal with a transparent and mastered functioning by its users" Poullet, "About the E-Privacy Directive: Towards a Third Generation of Data Protection Legislation?," 27. Such right, as heavily based on technological components and technical requisites embedded into terminal equipments, constitutes what I would call a derivation of the principle of technological assistance.

[144] Article 29 Data Protection Working Party (1999).

Protection Authorities holding terminal equipment manufacturers and information systems designers liable for legal violations linked to the design of their products.

1.7 Conclusion

In its Europe 2020 Strategy, the European Commission drew attention to "the fragmentation that currently blocks the flow of online content and access for consumers and companies"[145] within the envisaged digital single market, and emphasized the need to overcome it. Often in the offline world today, business and citizens still need to deal with 28 different legal systems for the same transaction.[146] We have attempted to demonstrate that there is still no specific legal framework for eID in the European Union. In the absence of a comprehensive framework, a loose amalgam of EU laws and member state legislation currently stand in to address issues pertaining to the protection and management of eIDs. Moreover, this legal patchwork is implemented and, to a certain extent, complemented by a series of technological initiatives and developments.

The EU's authority to enact an eID scheme is contentious and contested, while the EU legal taxonomy in this area is both immature and disintegrated. At present, European eID regulations are a hodgepodge of principles, rules, and concepts, borrowed from EU legal instruments and national laws, many of which were not conceived with the explicit intention of governing eID. In the absence of an integrated approach, member states regulate eID individually, though their approaches often conflict. Many member states have thus developed innovative technical and legal solutions in the absence of a comprehensive EU-level legal framework. As an example, and going beyond the applicability of their generic data protection regulations, a number of Member States have subjected some or all unique identifiers used in their administrations to additional protection mechanisms.[147] Impressive as these improvised legal and technical measures may be, they are not a suitable substitute for comprehensive, EU-level eID legislation.

In this chapter, we have contributed to the ongoing debate on the benefits of a pan-European regulatory framework for eID by presenting a number of legal proposals that could facilitate the realization of such a scheme. We have explored a number of new legal principles that take into account the unique dynamics of eID relative to conventional identification and the unique necessity for data protection and identity management that result from this unique disposition. These principles would form the hard core of a user-centric eID legal framework that empowers users to remain anonymous or employ pseudonyms online, where appropriate, to

---

[145] European Commission (2010d), p. 19.

[146] European Commission (2010d), p. 18.

[147] Graux et al. (2009), p. 115. Member States have also implicitly introduced in their legislation the already alluded authentic source principle.

effectively manage multiple identities and keep these identities separate from one another. These principles would further empower users to negotiate the terms by which third parties manage their identity data and to freely move their identity information between digital services, among other benefits. These principles would further enhance personal privacy online, bolster trust in digital interactions, and increase the confidence and security of digital transactions for vendors and consumers alike.

Technology is an important contributor to the practical realization of these principles but appropriate laws are ultimately required. We need a comprehensive legal framework that links member states into a seamless, fully interoperable eID regime that not only allows but also incentivizes electronic identities to unobtrusively travel across different EU member states, enabling access to services and transactions.

References

Andrade NNG (2011a) Data protection, privacy and identity: distinguishing concepts and articulating rights. In: Fischer-Hübner S, Duquenoy P, Hansen M, Leenes R, Zhang G (eds) Privacy and identity management for life: 6th Ifip Wg 9.2, 9.6/11.7, 11.4, 11.6/Primelife International Summer School, Helsingborg, 2–6 Aug 2010, Revised Selected Papers. Springer, Heidelberg, pp 90–107

Andrade NNG (2011b) The right to privacy and the right to identity in the age of ubiquitous computing: friends or foes? A proposal towards a legal articulation. In: Akrivopoulou C, Psygkas A (eds) Personal data privacy and protection in a surveillance era: technologies and practices. Information Science Publishing, Hershey, pp 19–43

Andrade NNG (2012a) Regulating electronic identity in the European Union: an analysis of the Lisbon Treaty's competences and legal basis for eID. Comp Law Secur Rev: Int J Technol Law Prac 28(2):152–163

Andrade NNG (2012b) Towards a European eID regulatory framework. Challenges in constructing a legal framework for the protection and management of electronic identities. In: Gutwirth S, De Hert P, Leenes R, Poullet Y (eds) European data protection: in good health?. Springer, Dordrecht, The Netherlands, pp 285–314

Article 29 Data Protection Working Party, "Recommendation 1/99 on Invisible and Automatic Processing of Personal Data on the Internet Performed by Software and Hardware," 1999

Craig P (2008) The treaty of Lisbon, process, architecture and substance. Eur Law Rev 33(2):137–166

Davis S (2009) A conceptual analysis of identity. In: Ian K, Valerie S, Carole L (eds) Lessons from the identity trail, p 213

Dumortier J (2003) Legal considerations with regard to privacy protection and identity management in the information society. 112e rapport annuel, Hochschüle für Technik und Architektur Biel, Tilt, no. 15:66–69

Dumortier J et al (2003) The legal and market aspects of electronic signatures, p 127. http://skilriki.is/media/skjol/electronic_sig_report.pdf

European Commission (2003) First report on the implementation of the data protection directive (95/46/Ec), Brussels

European Commission (2005) Signposts towards Egovernment 2010

European Commission (2006) Report of 15 March 2006 on the operation of directive 1999/93/EC on a community framework for electronic signatures, at 6, COM, 120 final (15 Mar 2006)

European Commission (2007) A roadmap for a Pan-European Eidm framework by 2010—V.1.0

European Commission (2010a) A comprehensive approach on personal data protection in the European Union. In: European Commission, Brussels

European Commission (2010b) A digital agenda for Europe. Brussels

European Commission (2010c) Delivering an area of freedom, security and justice for Europe's citizens: action plan implementing the Stockholm programme, Brussels

European Commission (2010d) Europe 2020: a strategy for smart, sustainable and inclusive growth, Brussels

European Commission (2010e) Towards interoperability for European public services

European Council (2010) Reflection group on the future of the EU 2030. Project Europe 2030. Challenges and Opportunities

Fearon JD (1999) What is identity (as we now use the word)? 4–5, 7 (unpublished manuscript). http://www.stanford.edu/~jfearon/papers/iden1v2.pdf. Accessed 3 Nov 1999

Froomkin MA (2011) Lessons learned too well (Miami Law Research Paper Series No. 2011-29) (unpublished manuscript). http://ssrn.com/abstract=1930017

Graux H, Majava J, Meyvis E (2009) Eid interoperability for pegs—update of country profiles—analysis and assessment report

Hildebrandt M (2008) Profiling and the identity of the European citizen. In: Mireille H, Serge G (eds) Profiling the European citizen 303

Jones A, Martin T (2010) Digital forensics and the issues of identity. Information security technical report, pp 1–5

Leenes R, Schallaböck J, Marit Hansen (2008) Prime (Privacy and Identity Management for Europe) White Paper

Leenes R, Priem B, van de Wiel C et al (2009) Stork—towards Pan-European recognition of electronic Ids (Eids) - D2.2—report on legal interoperability. STORK-eID Consortium, Den Haag

Modinis-IDM-Consortium (2005) Modinis study on identity management in Egovernment. Common terminological framework for interoperable electronic identity management—consultation paper V.2.01

Modinis-IDM-Consortium (2006) Modinis study on identity management in Egovernment, identity management issue interim report Ii1

Myhr T (2008) Legal and organizational challenges and solutions for achieving a pan-European electronic Id solution: or i am 621216-1318, but i am also 161262-43774. Do you know who i am? Information security technical report 13, no. 2, pp 76–82

Nabeth T (2009) Identity of identity. In: Kai R (eds) The future of identity in the information society: challenges and opportunities. Springer, Berlin, pp 19–69

OECD (2007) OECD recommendation on electronic authentication and OECD guidance for electronic authentication

OECD (2009) The role of digital identity management in the internet economy: a primer for policy makers

Ohm P (2009) Broken promises of privacy: responding to the surprising failure of anonymization. University of Colorado Law Legal Studies Research Paper No. 09–12

Pfitzmann A, Hansen M (2010) A terminology for talking about privacy by data minimization: anonymity, unlinkability, undetectability, unobservability, pseudonymity, and identity management (Version V0.34).

Poullet Y (2010) About the E-Privacy directive: towards a third generation of data protection legislation? In: Gutwirth S, Poullet Y, de Hert P (eds) Data protection in a profiled world. Springer Science + Business Media B.V, Dordrecht, pp 3–30

Rundle M (2006) International personal data protection and digital identity management tools, Berkman Center Research Publication No. 2006–06

van Rooy D, Bus J (2010) Trust and privacy in the future internet: a research perspective. Ident Inf Soc 3(2):397–404

Chapter 2
"eCert" Improving the Security and Controllability of Digitally Signed Documents

Lisha Chen-Wilson, David Argles, Michele Schiano di Zenise and Gary Wills

Abstract Issues and technology gaps exist in the realm of secure transmission of electronic documents. In this chapter, we propose a working solution ("eCert") to the problems identified. This has been developed by exploring a case study of an electronic qualification (eCertificate) system, by developing a prototype system, and by testing it within several popular ePortfolio systems. From this work, the underlying protocol (the "eCert protocol") has been abstracted and applied to a different domain, that of electronic identity documents. The resulting "Mobile eID" application has also been produced and tested, potentially enabling a person to carry their identity documents on a mobile phone, while ensuring that such documents can be verified as correct and tamper-free. A significant issue in this work is that the protocol developed is user-centric. Thus, the user retains ownership and control of their documents, yet is unable to tamper with the document contents, mirroring the current situation with corresponding paper equivalents.

Keywords eCert · eCertificate · ePortfolio · Mobile eID · eDocument · Digital signature · Security · User-centric · Owner control

2.1 Introduction

Paper-based certificates are still an important part of our study journeys in life. However, paper-based certificates have management problems; they can be easily lost or damaged, and they are hard to prove as genuine when presented.

In recent years, ePortfolio systems have become a major means for displaying academic achievements in the job and course application process. However, due to poor security, forged certificates can exist. Therefore, all claimed achievements within an ePortfolio should be verified. Professor Abrami, of the Centre for the Study

N. N. G. de Andrade et al., *Electronic Identity*, SpringerBriefs in Cybersecurity, DOI: 10.1007/978-1-4471-6449-4_2, © The Author(s) 2014

of Learning and Performance (CSLP) at Concordia University in Montreal, notes that it is difficult to authenticate the evidence in ePortfolios (Abrami and Barrett 2005).

While paper-based records and documents are gradually being digitized, concerns about how such electronic data are stored and transmitted have also increased. The traditional "Fortress Approach" to security, which uses a systems-orientated approach to protect against misuse from both outside attackers and uninformed legitimate users, is being challenged. The world within which users operate is changing—there is now a need to deal with peer-to-peer networking, social networking, and linked data. In this environment, the prevention of unauthorized modification and loss of records is vital. Such concerns are compounded by the knowledge that institutions that the public ought to be able to depend upon for maintaining the security of documents appear to have inadequate systems in place. In the UK, the government has been responsible for the loss of 10 million personal records that included bank account details (Sturcke 2007), and other examples exist of serious breaches of security protocol.

Besides the potential for human error, as noted above, there is also legitimate concern that confidential personal data could be passed to other organizations for financial gain. Without a system of checks and controls in place, there is no guarantee that confidential data will not be abused. In this context, it is understandable that information owners have increasing demands regarding their rights. As a result, there are now pressing calls for secure and user-centric systems in a wide range of domains, which aim to give owners the opportunity to choose where and how their information is collected and stored.

2.1.1 Digital Signing and Its Limitations

Reviewing existing eDocument-related security methods, such as water marks and locked PDF, the digital signing method proved to be most suitable for use in an eCertificate system. However, security issues exist in the field of encryption and digital signing (Kaliski 2003; Lysyanskaya 2002; Pfleeger and Pfleeger 2007; Mao 2004; Goldwasser et al. 1988), which define the limits of what can be achieved in an eCertificate system. Three main issues were identified. Among them, the validation of public key certificate status and eDocument content validation will directly affect the security of an eCertificate system. A new issue, eDocument status validation, which is critical to the eCertificate case, has not been mentioned in the literature. These three issues need to be addressed in eCertificate design in order to provide a secure eCertificate system.

2.1.1.1 Public Key Certificate Status Validation

A Certificate Revocation List (CRL) is a list of issued public key certificates that need to be revoked. The reasons for revocation can vary, but according to the revocation reason code specified in RFC 5280 (Network Working Group 2008), it is categorized as: *unspecified; keyCompromise; cACompromise; affiliationChanged; superseded; cessationOfOperation; certificateHold; removeFromCRL; privilege-Withdrawn; and aACompromise.*

When accessing a digitally signed eDocument, the system will automatically verify the integrity of the document by comparing the eDocument's hash value against the decrypted signature hash value. The reviewer will be informed if the signature is invalid (i.e., the two hash values do not match) (Kaliski 2003; Lysyanskaya 2002). However, not all systems will automatically check the status of the signature's signing key (the public key certificate) against the CRL. Some of them require the reviewer to manually open up the public key certificate to check the status when concerned, while some of them require the receiver to configure the system to enable the function.

In practice, a message may be displayed with a valid signature: "This document and all items contained in the document file are signed. All signatures are valid. Click here to view the signer's identity." Pronichkin commented that *CRL checking takes place on a per application basis, ... Some applications make verification failures visible to the user while other applications stay silent and suppress such messages* (Pronichkin ARTEM OR DIMITRY 2012). This is a known security hole; it can lead to documents signed by a revoked key being accepted, if this part of the verification process has been skipped.

2.1.1.2 eDocument Content Validation

The simplest form of signing is called Comprehensive Signing, where one or multiple signatures is used to sign all the content in a single document with no reference to external content. In addition, the eDocument contents have also been categorized in four additional groups relating to the different signing situations. These four groups are: unsigned content, signed content groups, externally referenced content, and dynamic content (Davis 2009). Signing for contents that fall into any of these four categories will invalidate the trust and should be avoided. *From a signature-trust standpoint, content that can be dynamically added, removed or altered is by its very nature unsignable.* When the situation is unavoidable, clear notifications should be provided (Davis 2009).

- For a document with pages/parts left unsigned or added later as unsigned parts, a verification result message should be displayed clearly to inform users of the unsigned but associated content.
- For a document with different signed content groups, a verification result message should be displayed clearly to inform users that signatures that relate to different content groups are independent.
- For a document with externally referenced content, a verification result message should be displayed clearly to enable the user to understand the situation and identify the unsigned external materials.

- For a document with dynamic content, such as inserted variable texts or results of running macros, a verification result message should be displayed clearly and accurately to enable the user to understand the situation and identify the unsigned dynamic materials.

Signed contents may be presented as being of various content types, such as text documents, media files, and program code. To accompany the various content types and signing categories, a digital signature with XML syntax has been defined, which can be used for signing data resources of any type and is most suitable for signing XML documents (Naedele 2003; W3C recommendation 2002). Three signing methods have been defined:

- a detached signature can be used for signing externally referenced resources;
- an enveloped signature can be used for signing part of the document;
- an enveloping signature can be used to sign a whole document and wrap the signed content within itself. This XML signature has the advantage over other forms of digital signatures, such as Pretty Good Privacy (PGP) (Zimmermann 1995) as it operates on the XML Infoset rather than binary data.

This allows various ways of binding the signature and the signed content (Naedele 2003; Selkirk 2001).

However, although the XML signature provides helpful signing methods, it still does not solve the security issue that arises when unsigned content is involved. This needs to be addressed when designing an eCertificate system.

2.1.1.3 eDocument Status Validation

After a long search in the literature, no information was found about revoking a signed document due to a changed situation so that the signed content is no longer true (there were lots information about revoking a digitally signed eDocument, but they were all about the signing key being compromised). This is similar to the situation with unsignable dynamic content that also involves some changes after signing, but the difference here is that the document can be a simple static file and perfectly signable.

Taking the eCertificate as an example, it could be a simple text file when it is signed, but what happens if fake evidence, or copied work, or cheating, has been discovered after the certificate has been issued? How can the eCertificate be revoked due to this changed situation but where the key has not been compromised? For the eCertificate, the public key certificate must be checked against the certificate revocation list (CRL) and also whether the content of the eCertificate, the qualification award certificate, has been withdrawn. Thus, the issues faced are of having two types of certificates to be verified: one well-documented and supported, and the other with no information at all. It might be called the (eCertificate)^2 (eCertificate-squared) issue.

2.1.2 Existing Systems Related to eCertificates

Before developing a new eCertificate system, it is important to find out what is currently available, what can be adapted, and what limitations need to be overcome. These, together with the literature review, will provide an informed background of what is required in the design of a new eCertificate system.

2.1.2.1 Europe: The Europass

The European Community provides Europass Certificate Supplements and Diploma Supplements (European Communities 2007), which are facsimiles of award certificates and information about the qualifications.[1] Europass was established in 2004, with the aim to *facilitate the mobility of European learners and workers by making their skills and qualifications more easily understood in Europe* (European Communities 2007). Besides the online CV, Europass offers four document services: Europass Language Passport; Europass Mobility; Europass Diploma Supplement; and Europass Certificate Supplement (European Communities 2007).

A Europass Certificate Supplement *is made available to individuals who hold a further education and training award certificate by the body that issued the award certificate.* It aims to make the award certificate *more easily understood by employers or institutions outside the issuing country. It provides additional information to the award certificate.* This includes (European Communities 2007):

- *the awarding status of the body that issued the award*
- *the skills and competences acquired by ALL holders of the award*
- *the level of the award in the national awarding system*
- *the typical entry requirements to programmes that lead to the award*
- *the typical employment or learning opportunities that are accessible to holders of the award.*

A Europass Diploma Supplement is issued with the degree or diploma certificate together. *It helps to ensure that higher education qualifications are more easily understood, especially outside the country where they were awarded* (European Communities 2007). It was developed by the European Commission, Council of Europe and UNESCO/CEPES and aims to provide *sufficient independent data to improve the international 'transparency' and fair academic and professional recognition of qualifications (diplomas, degrees, certificates, etc.)* It is designed to *provide a description of the nature, level, context, content, and status of the studies that were pursued and successfully completed by the individual*

---

[1] European Union. *Opening doors to learning and working in Europe: Information On Europass Certificate Supplement.* 2004; accessed on 28 January 2010; Available from: http://europass. cedefop.europa.eu/europass/home/hornav/Introduction.csp. All information about Europass was sourced from this website.

named on the original qualification to which the supplement is appended. The Diploma Supplement *is issued in a widely spoken European language and free of charge to every student upon graduation* (European Communities 2007).

The additional information provided with the award certificate, benefits both the award certificate holders and the reviewers (European Communities 2007):

- *award holders will be able to communicate their qualifications and competences in an effective way*
- *employers will find the qualifications and competences of job-seekers easier to understand*
- *education and training providers and guidance counsellors will find it easier to provide accurate advice to award holders regarding suitable learning opportunities.*

The Europass clearly states that, *The Europass Certificate Supplement is not a substitute for the original certificate* or *an automatic system that guarantees recognition* (European Communities 2008).

2.1.2.2 China: The HEQC

In China, an online information verification service for higher education qualification certificates (HEQC) has been running since 2001. The service is carried out by the China Higher Education Student Information and Career Centre (CHESICC). It is based on information collected since 1991.[2]

CHESICC is *a specialized body authorized by the Chinese Ministry of Education (CME) for verifying any certificates or diplomas awarded in China* (CHESICC 2008). Its website is the sole website designated by the CME for HEQC inquiries. It has the only database for information of the HEQC.

The service provides online certificate information, verification for those certificates that were gained in higher education since 2001, and an offline certificate verification service for any year's certificates. The certificates that have been verified offline will then be also available for online verification. The service is designed for individuals as well as organizations.

The government announced that every student who started their HE course since 2001 must have an electronic student status registration. The students who have an electronic status registration record will be able to register their certificate information and build it up in their years of study. Both the student status and the certificate information are verified step by step under the management of the government body. The certificates that were awarded before 2001 will require offline certificate certification before they can be available for the online verification service.

---

[2] CHESICC. *The Certificate Information Verification services in China.* 2005; accessed on 02 September 2008; Available from: http://www.chsi.com.cn/about_en/. All information about CHESICC was sourced from this website.

The system is implemented on a big scale in both time and coverage, and the government authorized body provides the trust. The whole process sounds like creating an ePortfolio (with the student status as the ePortfolio account and the certificate information as its contents), but it is at a government level, not a personal level, so that the student (the account holder) has no control in the use of it. The service targets verification only, not the wider uses of eCertification that is the focus of this research.

2.1.2.3 ROI: Digitary

Digitary, which stands for "Digital Notary", was established by Framework Solutions in 1999. It worked with the Higher Education sector, to issue, distribute, and authenticate official electronic graduation documents over the Internet.[3] It was first implemented in 2005 (Digitary 2008).

Digitary describes itself as *a high-security software system developed with the Higher Education sector for the online issuing and authentication of tamper-evident electronic official graduation documents* (Digitary 2008). It also states that documents issued through the system are electronically signed by officials of issuing institutions and are therefore legally valid.

Digitary is the "trading name of Framework Computer Consultants Limited, registered in the Republic of Ireland." Educational institutions who want to use the service need to install the system on their site, and students need to login to their institution's system to access their documents. Employers, who want to verify qualifications that were sent by the students or graduates, "are required to carry out registration" on Digitary at the issuing institutions, in order to authenticate and view the documents (Digitary 2008).

Students who "have been issued with Digitary documents by their institutions" can allocate "rights for who can access them by emailing a Document Access Ticket to them. People who have been given the right to access can authenticate and view documents". People who receive Document Access Tickets may also need to complete an online account registration process if restrictions were set by the student. When an employer or third party verifies a Digitary document through the system, it performs a number of security checks on the document; that:

- they have been granted access to the document by the owner;
- the document has not been revoked for any reason;
- the document was issued by authorized officials of the institution in question;
- the document has not been tampered with in any way.

---

[3] Digitary. *Secure Electronic Documents*. 2008; accessed on 16 August 2008; Available from: http://www.digitary.net/aboutus.htm. All information about Digitary was sourced from this website.

Employers need to make separate registrations with every institution's system where the qualifications were originally issued, to be able to verify the documents.

2.1.2.4 Research System: The eCert-GDP2008 Project

A project entitled "eCert-GDP2008" (Royce et al. 2008) ran in the school of Electronics and Computer Science, at the University of Southampton, exploring the issues of online authentication of awards, and producing an award verification demonstrator. It explored the issues of three-party authentication and demonstrated how best to approach the process of validating students', claimed awards in such an environment. EdExcel, a UK national certifying authority, was also involved in working with the project team to explore and create a potential model and proof-of-concept system.

The eCert-GDP2008 project raised interesting points. In particular, many conventional security scenarios assume two stakeholder transactions, with any third party involved being an attacker. In the GDP2008 project, eCertification has three parties involved in the transaction; any external attacker becomes a fourth party. The system not only dealt with access to resources with the attendant issues of Authorization, but also with verification of the information provided. The group made some security policy decisions. These not only concern who can see what and when, but also what the value of the data concerned is. For example, one might decide that information about qualifications is less valuable than banking details, so the level of security could be lower if it aids usability of the system. In contrast, one might decide that the level of security should be higher to prevent identity theft, for example. The security policy decisions adopted were (Royce et al. 2008):

- *The data is to be regarded as important and therefore should be properly secured*
- *There should be minimal transfer of data*
- *It should not be possible to browse the data; all queries should be of the format, < claimed award > and the response, < true/false>*
- *The award holder (student) should determine who may see their award details.*

These decisions introduced novel design criteria. The basic concept was that there would be a Certification Server—the Certifying Authority in the original design. This provides a service to the ePortfolio Holder (student) who can build up a set of ePortfolio certificates, each one tailored for a specific ePortfolio Reviewer (e.g., employer). Because of design policy 3 above, it is not possible for the student to browse their awards and select from a list, rather they have to be entered individually. Although this could be annoying for the student, it prevents attackers from intercepting the communication and obtaining all the student's qualifications in one go. Similarly, it prevents the employer from taking the student's details and making a general enquiry to see what information about awards has been withheld.

2.1.2.5 System Comparison and Analysis

The systems described above provide services for signing and/or verifying online qualification records or eDocuments. However, they are built with specific applications in mind, and do not satisfy the more general requirements for eCertificates. This is summarized below and compared in Table 2.1.

- The eCert-GDP2008 project only verifies input qualification records against linked institutional databases but does not involve eCertificates, therefore the paper-based certificate management issues remain unsolved.
- The Europass Certificate Supplement and a Diploma Supplement only provide facsimiles of award certificates and information about the qualification. It does not guarantee validity.
- The Chinese Certificate Information Verification service is an eCertification service for qualification records, similar to eCert-GDP2008, but not a platform for student owners to manage their own eCertificates.
- The Digitary system is the closest system to the research criteria, however, it is heavily reliant on the issuing institution. Lifelong validation of the issued eCertificate would be a problem if anything happens to the institution (e.g., it closes down) or its database (e.g., being hacked).

2.1.3 Domain Expert Advice

Nottingham University is one of the leading research groups in ePortfolio studies. The university provided expert reviewers for the eCert-GDP2008 project, an e-certification project for qualification records. Feedback on ePortfolio operations was also supplied as secondary data for the project.

Expert review was also provided at an early stage of this research to collect professional opinions on the new eCertificate system. As the topic was new to both parties, no specific requirements were noted at that time. However, concerns were raised, such as potential file size of the certificates and the nature and role of such a system. Advice was that for the new eCertificate system to be a success, these concerns need to be addressed in the design stage.

2.1.4 The Challenges and Plan

From the issues and requirements mentioned above, an ideal eCertificate system presents special challenges such as:

Table 2.1 eCertificate-related systems comparison

	Verify eCertificate	Verification nationwide	Require system storage	User control usage	Solve (certificate)[2] problem	Provide lifetime validation
The GDP2008 project	No, records of awards only	Yes/No (for linked institutions' only)	Little (plus access to linked institutions' database)	N/A	N/A	No
The Chinese system	No, records of awards only	Yes	Medium (record only)	N/A	N/A	Yes (reported and stored in central)
Digitary	Yes	Yes/No (for installed institution only)	Huge (eDocs, access controls, and histories for each account)	Yes	No info	Not guaranteed, depend on the issuing institution.
Europass	Yes	Yes	Little	No	No	No

- The inclusion of nonstatic content—not only may the signing key be compromised, its content (the award qualification) may be withdrawn;
- Owner control demands—the student, as the owner of the eCertificate, need to have control over its usage;
- Lifelong availability requirements—verifiable throughout a student's lifetime, not just the lifetime of the issuing authority.

Although digital signatures are being used in eDocuments to provide authentication, integration, and nonrepudiation, and while currently there are many commercial systems offering eDocument signing services, at present it appears that traditional digital signature systems and existing commercial systems provide no method for the following:

- Checking whether content revocation is in place—it only checks the signing key revocation;
- Independent user-centric control—third party access control of an eCertificate needs to rely on the support systems of either the issuing institution or of the signing service provider. In this case, a re-signing process will need to take place to generate a distinct access key. However, the owner still has no control over the distributed eCertificates, which may in turn be passed on without the owner's consent.
- Lifelong availability—At present, this relies on the issuing institution's or service provider's willingness to hold the certificate over time and the guarantee that the organization remains in business.

The problems that the public are facing need answers. In order to solve the current paper-based certificate management issue and satisfy the requirement of validating the claimed achievements in an ePortfolio, while also addressing the increasing eDocument privacy issue and answer the calls for enhanced owner control, it is necessary to design a secure eCertificate system that is as acceptable as paper-based certificates and which can be verified in a legal context. It needs to be available throughout the student owner's life, be able to be withdrawn, and to be used either as a standalone application or as a service within other applications, such as ePortfolios. The student, as the owner of an eCertificate, needs to have ownership rights and to be able to control its usage. Such an eCertificate also needs to be easy to use and to suit users with low IT skill levels while maintaining high levels of security to prevent forgery and to provide a verification service. We need to secure the eCertificate system, not just the eCertificate alone.

It is believed that current technology is available to design and implement such an eCertificate system, and that the concept of the eCertificate solution can be applied to other eDocument-related domains that face similar complex situations, such as eID or eContract, solving their security and ownership issues. Therefore, this research was planned in three steps:

1. use eCertificate as a case study to research a solution for the eDocument security and controllability problem;
2. design and build a demonstration system to test and evaluate the design and prove the first part of the hypothesis;
3. apply the eCertificate solution to another eDocument transmitting case and test the use of the eCertificate concept in a wider eDocument transmitting domain.

To make the research process efficient, the principles of research methodology have been studied. Multiple methods can provide a better view into a research topic (Saunders et al. 2009), and since the goal of this research is to understand the issues and find a solution for the problem rather than measuring and benchmarking a proposed system, a software development research methodology, Service Orientated Reference Model (SORM) (Wills et al. 2006) has been selected to investigate the eCertificate framework. A qualitative based research methodology, Delphi (Linstone and Turoff 2002), has been identified to guide and evaluate the eCertificate system design alongside the SORM methodology.

- The SORM methodology was used to develop the eCertificate case study, from its use case, gap analysis, and services investigation, through to system design and implementation.
- In parallel with the SORM methodology, the Delphi methodology was employed step-by-step alongside the eCertificate system development. Domain experts' opinions were collected and analyzed to guide the system design decisions.

2.2 Development of the eCertificate System

The domain definition layer has been explored in Sect. 2.1. Following the SORM methodology, an eCertificate case study was carried out for the next layer: the use cases. This section describes the formal use cases and the processes that lie between the related layers, the common usage patterns, and the gap analysis. These involve summarizing key activities from the domain, identifying the eCertificate stakeholders, developing use cases where these stakeholders act, while considering techniques that address similar issues through a gap analysis.

2.2.1 Common Usage Patterns

From the study of domain definition, key activities for the eCertificate domain have been identified. As a result, the common usage patterns have been generated as requirements for the new eCertificate system, and these are summarized in Table 2.2.

Table 2.2 Common usage patterns as eCertificate system requirements (SR)

SR Identity	Summary
SR-01	Can be used stand-alone or served within an ePortfolio
SR-02	Security control throughout the whole eCertificate lifecycle: from generation, issue, distribution, to verification; involves hardware, software, database, information, and human control
SR-03	Can be verified in a legal context, supports withdrawal of an eCertificate and the content status validation as well as the signing key status validation
SR-04	Ensure that the owner has control over the usage of their eCertificates
SR-05	Effective usage: easy to use, supports lifetime validation, and can be widely verified and recognized throughout the UK

2.2.2 Stakeholder Analysis

In ePortfolio systems, an ePortfolio is considered to have two stakeholders: the ePortfolio creator as the owner, and receiver as the reviewer. In eWork,[4] the qualification data is considered to have three stakeholders: the record creator as the issuer, a government body as the holder/owner, the student and any third parties who need access as the reviewer (Macnamara et al. 2010, 2011).

In this study, the eCertificate owner is considered to be the student graduate, just like the ownership that they have of their paper-based certificates. According to studies of related systems, the eCertificate system is considered to have three stakeholders: the originating institution as the issuer, the student as the owner, and the receiver as the reviewer. Any government bodies that co-own the qualification records are not considered as eCertificate owners. Likewise they do not own the students' paper-based certificates. However, the proposed eCertificate could record, hold, and provide access to any government bodies, as it will be able to be used on its own or as a service within other systems. These three stakeholders perform three processes: issue, distribute, and verify, as showed in Fig. 2.1.

2.2.3 Use Case

Based on the certificate process study from the literature review, with the selected three eCertificate stakeholders in mind, and the user case collation (Higgs et al. 2010) from the eWork project, the related personas and scenarios have been arranged to help with understanding the situation. Through the scenarios and use case study, it was noted that the eCertificate system involves assertion, trust, privacy, distribution, property rights, and lifetime issues.

---

[4] In 2009, the Department of Education, Employment and Workplace Relations of the Australian government established the Australian Flexible Learning Framework, and set up the eWork project to *investigate existing learner information verification services and systems* to *identify the verification needs of third parties* (Macnamara et al. 2010, 2011).

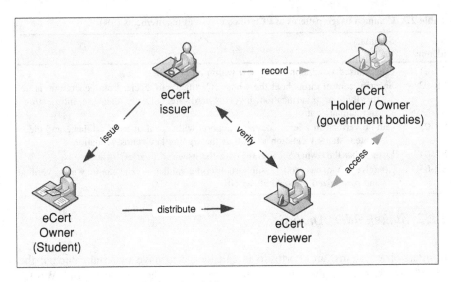

Fig. 2.1 eCertificate stakeholders and activities

- eCertificate assertion: the system needs to be self-certificating to prove it is genuine; and to allow reviewers to verify it; and for the issuers to withdraw it.
- eCertificate privacy: the requirement of being able to tailor an ePortfolio to best support the owner's application also applies to eCertificates, as our aim is to give students control over who can see their eCertificates and for how long. This can also prevent misuse of the eCertificate without the owner's permission.
- Information property rights: owners have the ownership right of their qualification attainments, in the same way as paper-based certificates. They should have the right to store, manage, share, and track, "under their control, with their consent, and for their benefit".
- Stakeholder trust: the need to establish trust among all three stakeholders is a fundamental requirement, so that one stakeholder can have faith that the identity of another is true.
- Distributed stakeholders: the eCertificate system needs to define an *architecture of participation* to *stimulate large-scale uptake* of users, as the system will not work without a significant body of universities and employers involved.
- eCertificate lifetime validation: an issued eCertificate needs to remain verifiable throughout the student's lifetime even when the issuing institution does not exist any more.

2.2.4 Gap Analysis

With the use cases defined, a gap analysis against current techniques was carried out to discover which technical gaps need to be addressed.

2.2.4.1 Gaps in Related Technology

The literature review for encryption and eDocument security techniques, such as password locked PDF, watermarking,[5] and digital signature, showed that among these existing eDocument security techniques, digital signing could be the most suitable one for an electronic version of qualification certificate (eCertificate). It "is a mathematical scheme" for "authentication of a digital message or document" (Lysyanskaya 2002; Rivest et al. 1978). It not only detects unauthorized modification, but also proves the issuer, and therefore provides trust that the eDocument is genuine. However, the literature review also indicated that some limitations exist, such as service support, key management, and lifelong validation. These crucial limitations affect its security efficiency when applied to an eCertificate system, especially for an eCertificate that may contain nonstatic contents, and which needs to be transferred to three or more parties.

Access support and owner control: As computing technology developed, the concerns of data privacy and eDocument ownership rights intensified. It has been noted that an eDocument owner has the right to "store, manage, share and track" their personal data, "under their control, with their consent, and for their benefit" (Sadd 2010). Unlike paper-based documents that can be presented anywhere, digitally signed eDocuments are currently based on organizations for its service support, so that the reviewer can only verify it through the organization-provided service. Many organizations also provide access control functions for stored e-Documents through a system to confirm the ownership right, such as Digitary. However, this method depends heavily on the issuing body, in the case of the eCertificate, it is inconvenient for a reviewer to verify the eDocuments through many different systems, since they will have eCertificates issued by many different organizations. Moreover, should anything happen to the issuing organization, e.g., going out of business, or database being damaged, this will result in the eDocument becoming invalid. This lifelong validation issue is crucial to an eCertificate as a genuine eCertificate must remain valid even if the issuing body no longer exists.

eDocument content validation: digital signed eDocument content can be presented in various forms, such as unsigned content, signed content groups, externally referenced content, and dynamic content. It may also contain various content types, such as text documents, media files, and program code. To accompany the various content types and forms, a digital signature with XML syntax was defined. It has three signing methods: detached signature, enveloped signature, and

---

[5] Locked PDF and water marking are commonly used in protecting digital data from unauthorized access and copying. *By embedding a cryptographic string, or water mark, a legitimate author can demonstrate the origin of the file* (Pfleeger and Pfleeger 2007); However, simple locked PDF can be easily unlocked through password recovery software; and although these techniques could be used to protect unauthorized copying, accessing, and to indicate who the issuer is, for use in eCertificate case, it could not prove that the issuer was an authorized educational body and they don't handle the withdraw process.

enveloping signature, each designed to handle the various content forms. However, the content of an eCertificate will not solely comprise one content type or form, but a combination of them. For example, the evidence file could be the externally referenced content, the transits file and the qualification file could become the signed content groups, and the qualification award itself is the dynamic content as it may be withdrawn at a later stage. What is more, there is no specification of how an eCertificate file should be structured and how it should be verified. Therefore, how to combine the different XML signing methods together to sign the various content types and forms to ensure the security and trust becomes the main technical gap that needs to be overcome.

eDocument content status validation: digital signing is most suited to signing static eDocuments, but not to eDocuments with changing status, as it only validates the eDocument's content modification and the status of the signer's public key certificates (PKC), without validating the status of the document's actual content. This is crucial to an eCertificate as this signed eDocument itself is also a certificate, which may have a valid period (e.g., first aid certificate), and may be revoked in a later stage (e.g., if plagiarism is discovered). The problem we are dealing with is a certificate squared issue, referred to as (certificate)^2 issue, which involves the issuer's PKC and the qualification certificate as a whole.

Auto request of signing key status validation: Current Public Key Infrastructure (PKI) does not start the validation of the public key certificate's status automatically. It will only undertake this process if required. In the case of an eCertificate, this is a critical security hole as it may result in a forgery being accepted if the key has been compromised.

2.2.4.2 Technical Requirements

Referring to the system requirements summarized from the domain definition and common usage pattern, the corresponding technical requirements from the use case study and gap analysis are listed in Table 2.3. They will then need to be addressed and reflected in the design of the new system.

2.2.5 Service Profile

With the use cases defined and a gap analysis produced, the next step in following the SORM methodology is to develop a complete service profile. Hence, techniques to tackle the issues were investigated to discover what existing services can be reused or adopted and what new services are required.

- Existing Services
  - Service Orientated Architecture (SOA): offers greater interoperability between systems and software across the eLearning community; provides

Table 2.3 Technical requirements (TR)

SR ID	TR ID	Summary
SR-01	TR-01	System adaptability and compatibility so that the system can be embedded as a plug-in within other systems, e.g., eFolio
SR-02	TR-02	Security control: include hardware, database, and network
	TR-03	System access control for students, reviewers, and any third parties
	TR-04	eCertificate access control for students, reviewers, and any third parties
SR-03	TR-05	Support content modification validation
	TR-06	Support withdrawal of an eCertificate
	TR-07	Support revocation of the signing key
	TR-08	Can verify and prove issuer
SR-04	TR-09	The student owner of the eCertificate can have control over who can see it and for how long, without the need of re-signing by the issuer
SR-05	TR-10	Stimulate large-scale uptake, enabling eCertificate to be widely verified and recognized throughout the UK
	TR-11	Support lifetime validation, can be independent from the issuing body
	TR-12	Easy to use, suits low IT skill users, both students and reviewers
	TR-13	Minimize system storage
	TR-14	Establish stakeholder trust between all involved parties

an architecture for participation (Papazoglou 2003); and hence could be used to address the distributed stakeholder use case.

- Digital signing: provides authentication, integrity, and nonrepudiation, which could be used to address part of the eCertificate assertion use case. Its CAs provide a chain of trusted nodes which could be used to address part of the stakeholder trust use case.
- Federated Identity: the open-source federated identity system Shibboleth (Hartnell-Young et al. 2006) could be used to address another part of the stakeholder trust use case so that "a home user identity is valid at any of the partner institutions within the federation" (Saunders et al. 2009).

- Services Required

  - Stakeholder trust: Although the identities of eCertificate owners could be validated by adapting Shibboleth, and digital signing can provide the stakeholder trust as the CAs provide a chain of trusted nodes, we still require services to provide trust between all stakeholders, especially when the eCertificate is transmitted to three or more receivers, where extra care of key management and service support are involved.

- Unique ID system: we need to have a unique student id system and certificate id system established nationwide.
- Access control: eCertificate owners need to have control over who can see what and for how long.
- Lifetime Validation: eCertificates need to be verifiable even if the issuing institution does not exist years later.

- Bridging the Gap

  - XML Signatures: By adopting XML signatures, combining the detached and enveloped method, we can use detached signatures to sign any eCertificate related support documents, and then use the enveloped signature to sign the whole eCertificate with the detached signature value embedded. This will meet the assertion use case for any information involved in an eCertificate.
  - XML metadata: employing the detached and enveloped signatures to digitally sign an eCertificate and its metadata.
  - A timestamp: enhancing the integrity of the signature.
  - Auto verification of CRLs: validating as a certificate against the public key revocation list and the qualification award Certificate Revocation List.

2.2.6 Approaches for Meeting the Requirements

Based on the service profiles and the ideas for bridging the gap, design approaches (DA) to meet the requirements have been drawn up. They are summarized in Table 2.4.

2.2.7 System Structure Development

Although digital signing is widely used for verifying eDocuments, it is more suitable for a "one stop" situation. When applying it to a "multiple stops" situation, a system needs to be designed to handle the trust issue, such as the keys and their related security problems.

2.2.7.1 Approach 1: Existing Transmission Process

If a digitally signed document is used to replace the paper-based document within the existing issue, distribute, and verify process path, as shown in Fig. 2.2, it raises many issues. The two main ones are:

- *Service support to handle the digitally signed documents: An efficient way to prove the issue of an eDocument is to have it digitally signed. However, this*

Table 2.4 Design approaches (DA)

TR ID	DA ID	Summary
TR-01	DA-01	Use XML to enable easy transaction between systems with different platforms
TR-02	DA-02	The eCertificate generation and issuing process, the hardware, database, and network security, and human control for both staff and students, will be guarded by the issuing body
TR-03	DA-03	Adapt Federated Identity system technique; access control to the eCertificate system will be based on system roles
TR-04	DA-04	Access control to eCertificates will be restricted to authorized users only
TR-05	DA-05	Employ digital signing to support content modification validation
TR-06	DA-06	Design a new function for eCertificate content status validation, address the unique eCertificate squared problem, support withdrawal of an eCertificate
TR-07	DA-07	Design a new function to support the auto verification of signing key CRL
TR-08	DA-08	Design a new structure for eCertificate so that it can contain the various information files which can be legally accepted and verified
	DA-09	Adapt the XML signature technique to support the verification of the various information types involved in an eCertificate
	DA-10	Employ a timestamp technique to enhance the signature integrity
TR-09	DA-11	Employ XML metadata for eCertificate access control values
	DA-12	Design a new signing method that allows the modification of eCertificate metadata while maintaining the integrity of the digital signature, so that the student owner can set access control to an eCertificate without the need for re-signing by the issuer
TR-10	DA-13	Adapt SOA to provide an architecture for participation which will enable large-scale uptake
	DA-14	Adapt a national unique number system to enable the eCertificate system to be rolled out throughout the UK
TR-11	DA-15	An independent system to provide the required services
TR-12	DA-16	Provide functions with a user-friendly interface to deal with complicated technical requirements, such as key management
TR-13	DA-17	Avoid storing sensitive data, minimize system storage to reduce the attraction of database attacks
TR-14	DA-18	Employ PKI to establish stakeholder trust between all involved parties

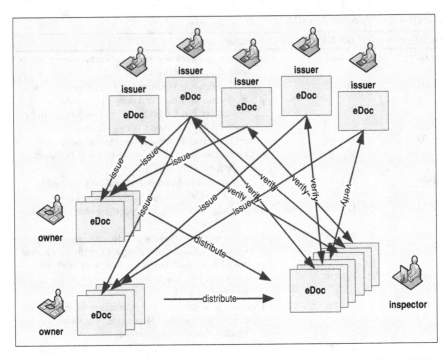

Fig. 2.2 Transmitting eDocuments with existing processes, published in (Chen-Winson 2010)

requires all the receivers (the eDocument owner and all inspectors) to have service support to handle the verification process. They will need to have the relevant IT skills to manage the operation, especially for the first time if system setup is required. As different institutions will use different methods to sign their eDocuments, this may require all receivers to have services for each issuing institution.

- *Privacy and Confidentiality issues: If an inspector has the service support (with the public key) for a selected issuer, this may mean that the inspector can view any eDocuments signed by this issuer; if these services are publicly available for inspectors (and anyone could be an inspector), this may mean that everyone can access any digitally signed documents, including stolen ones. There is no way for the users to have control over their usage. This is strictly against the confidentiality and privacy requirement.*

2.2.7.2 Approach 2: Institution-Based Transmission

There could be an institution based approach, as shown in Fig. 2.3, taking the Digitary system as an example. (a) eDocuments stored in the issuer's system; (b) The issuer also provides an online support service for eDocument management and

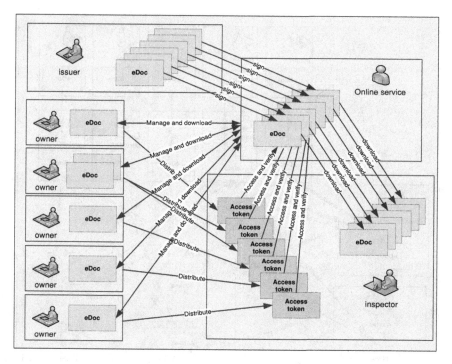

Fig. 2.3 Transmitting with an institution approach, published in (Chen-Winson 2010)

verification; (c) the owners can access the online management system to set access control for their own eDocument before sending out the link and access token to the specified inspector; d) the inspector can access the online verification system through the link and use the access token to view, verify, and download the eDocument.

This approach addresses the privacy and confidentiality issues by setting access tokens. Therefore, the inspectors can only access the ones that they have the tokens for. However, some issues have arisen:

- *Privacy and Confidentiality issue: The access token only controls the first time round. Once the inspector has accessed the online system and downloaded the eDocument, the owner will have lost control of it afterwards.*
- *System storage: This approach requires huge storage as it needs to store all the issued eDocuments for a lifetime.*
- *Lifetime validation: This approach relies heavily on the institution (the issuer). Lifetime validation is a problem if the institution no longer exists.*

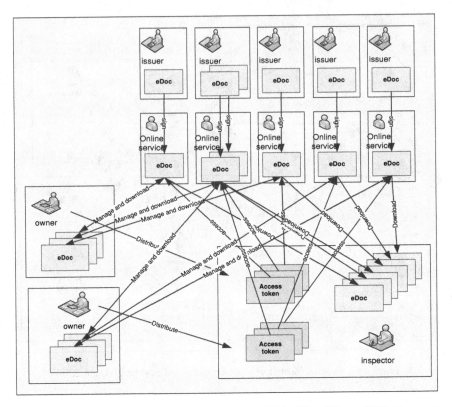

Fig. 2.4 Usage issue of the institution approach, published in (Chen-Winson 2010)

- *Security: The information stored is considered as high value and sensitive. The support service provides an active channel to the backend database, which could increase the risk of attacks.*
- *Usage: It is inconvenient for the inspector when eDocuments are issued from many different institutions, as shown in* Fig. 2.4.

2.2.7.3 Approach 3: Central Service and Storage

Taking the Chinese system as an example, a central service approach, as shown in Fig. 2.5, could be provided. (a) a central online system provides the management and verification service for all institutions that have joined; (b) all institutions issue eDocuments using the same standard, which are then uploaded to the central system; (c) the owners can access the online management system to set access control of their own eDocument before sending out the link and access token to the specified inspector; (d) the inspector can access the online verification system through the link and use the access token to view, verify, and download the eDocument.

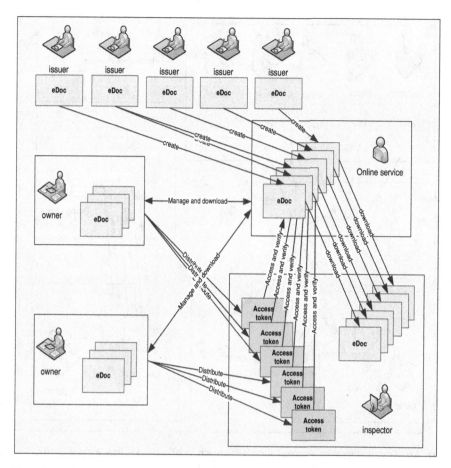

Fig. 2.5 Transmitting with a central storage approach, published in (Chen-Winson 2010)

Compared to the institution approach, this approach addresses the lifetime validation issue, and also solves the inconvenience problem as the inspectors only need to access one reference point for all the eDocuments. However, it requires an even bigger store, and increases the risk of database attacks as it now has a much bigger database.

- *System storage: This approach requires huge storage as it need to store all the eDocuments issued for a lifetime.*
- *Security: This approach stores all issued eDocuments from institutions that have joined into one backend database, the risk of being attacked is considered very high.*
- *Trust: Who will host such a system? It must be trusted by all institutions as it holds the information for all of them. The English government has a history of losing sensitive information, and in some cases, the whole database.*

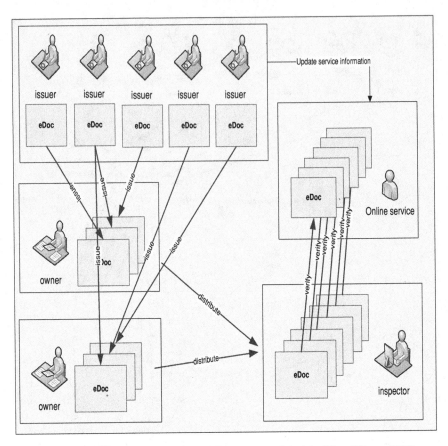

Fig. 2.6 Transmitting with a central service approach, published in (Chen-Winson 2010)

2.2.7.4 Approach 4: Central Service Only

As the central storage in approach 3 above causes lots of problems, perhaps a central service approach without storing the eDocument in the system, as shown in Fig. 2.6, would suffice. (a) a central online system provides the management and verification service for all institutions that have joined; (b) all institutions issue eDocuments using the same standard, which are then sent to the owners; (c) the owners can access the online management system to set access control of their own eDocuments before sending out to the inspector; and (d) the inspector accesses the online verification system to verify the eDocument.

Compared to the approach of central service with stored eDocuments, this approach solves the three issues that the other one faced: (a) it does not require storage for the eDocuments; (b) the eDocuments are not stored in one system, thus reducing the attack risk factor dramatically; (c) the eDocuments are not stored in one system, so there will be no risk of data being lost, therefore it will be much easier to find a body to run the service that everyone can agree on. However, this approach brings back the three way transmitting situation, and again face the keys management, privacy and confidentiality issues described earlier.

- *Privacy and Confidentiality issue: In this approach, an inspector can have the service support for all issuers. If the inspector has the public key for one eDocument, he can access all eDocuments issued by that issuer. If the inspector can get hold of one eDocument from each issuer, then he can access any eDocuments, including stolen ones. This is strictly against the confidentiality and privacy requirement.*

2.2.7.5 The Chosen Approach

As the approach of an online central service—without storing eDocuments—meets most of the major requirements, it has therefore been selected as a basis for the system structure design.

- *Pros:*

  - System storage: it does not store eDocuments on the central system, saving huge storage;
  - Security: as sensitive data is not stored in the system, many attacks can be avoided;
  - Trust: The central system is only there to provide a service, as the sensitive data is not stored in the system, there will be no risk of the data being lost. People in general, do not trust government bodies holding their personal data, so this approach makes having such a central system a possibility.
  - Usage: convenient for the inspectors to access eDocuments from a wide range of issuers.
  - Lifetime validation: independent central system, can valid eDocuments even when the issuer no longer exists.

- *Cons:*

  - Privacy and Confidentiality issue: an inspector can have the service support for all issuers. If the inspector has the public key for one eDocument, he can access all eDocuments issued by that issuer. If the inspector can get hold of one eDocument from each issuer, then he can access any eDocuments. This is strictly against the confidentiality and privacy requirement. It is the main issue that still needs to be addressed.
  - Issues noted in the gap analysis still need to be addressed.

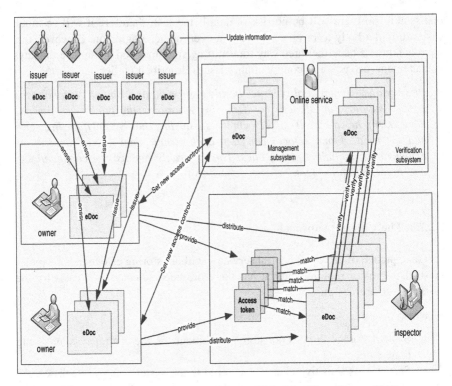

Fig. 2.7 The new eDocument transmitting design, published in (Chen-Winson 2010)

2.2.7.6 The eCert System Structure Design

The proposed solution is shown in Fig. 2.7. (a) a central online system provides the management and verification service for all institutions that have joined; (b) all institutions issue eDocuments using the same standard, document signed using the issuer's private key, the metadata that contains the access token, and the whole XML document will be signed using the owner's public key, the file is then sent to the owners; (c) the owners can access the online management system to set new access control of their own eDocument before sending out to the inspector; and (d) the inspector accesses the online verification system to verify the eDocument.

2.2.8 Core Design

The system design focuses on four areas: the eCert file structure, the system structure, the signature method, and the authentication and verification processes.

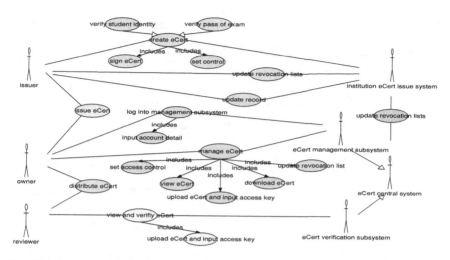

Fig. 2.8 eCert system design in use case diagram, published in (Chen-Winson 2010)

2.2.8.1 Systems and Relationships

The eCertificate system (eCert) will be constructed in two parts: an issuing system and an online central system.

The online central system will also be constructed in two parts: a management subsystem (for students) and a verification subsystem (for reviewers). It will provide services for eCertificates issued from any involved institutions, and will be the single reference point nationwide. This will prevent confusion to reviewers of not knowing which system to choose or which can be trusted, especially when they have lots of eCertificates issued from different institutions. This will also have the advantage of having close monitoring and control against fake systems.

The issuing system will be installed at individual institutions. The institution creates and issues digitally signed and access-controlled eCertificates to the specified students through the local issuing system. The students view and set new access controls on the received eCertificates through the central management system before sending them out to further reviewers. The reviewers use the central verification system to view and verify the access-controlled eCertificate. This is shown as a use case diagram in Fig. 2.8. The procedure for the issue, distribution, and verification processes between the stakeholders and the service support systems is shown as a sequence diagram in Fig. 2.9.

2.2.8.2 File Structure

An eCertificate contains three files: a qualification award file, providing qualification award details that a paper-based certificate would offer; a transcript file, providing the related course and institution information so that the qualification

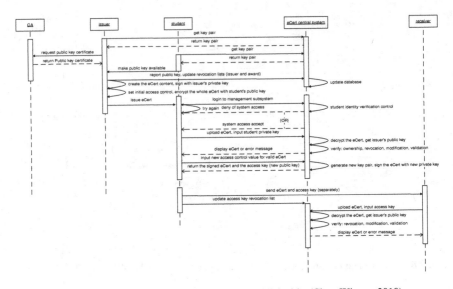

Fig. 2.9 eCert system design in sequence diagram, published in (Chen-Winson 2010)

can be well understood; and any evidence files if applicable, providing the information that the assessment was based on. An evidence file can be in any format, and can be seen as proof of the skill as it is bound with the awarded qualification. An eCertificate file will be a compressed file of these three files with their access metadata, and the signer's signature information.

To ensure that the eCertificate owner has the right to control the usage of the document, the transcript file and the evidence files will be set as optional for display, while the qualification award file will be compulsory at all times. The system will enable the eCertificate owner to select the preferred section(s) and set an access time limit for individual reviewers to best fit their various purposes. The metadata will contain the section display values and access time limit, as well as the eCertificate ID, student ID, and certificate expiry date. The section display values for the transcript file and the evidence file will be set to *true*, and the access time value will be set to *unlimited* by default on issue. All values in the metadata will be verified, and the eCertificate will be regarded as invalid if it fails to pass any of the verification processes. The controlled eCertificate will be encrypted individually, so that only the person with the given corresponding decryption key can access it.

2.2.8.3 The eCert Signature

Simple digital signatures are not secure enough for signing the eCert file due to its special file structure. With the traditional method, an enveloped signature can be used to sign the qualification award file, and the detached signature can be used to

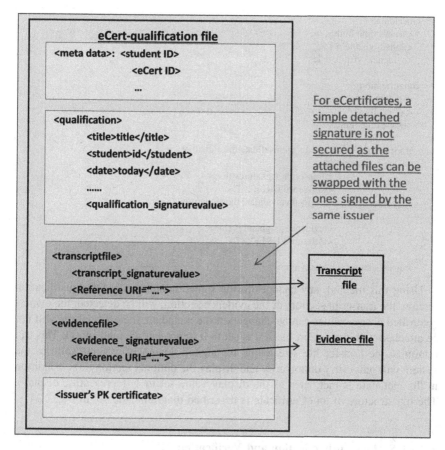

Fig. 2.10 Issues when applying the traditional signature method directly

sign the attached transcript file and evidence file. However, by using this method, individual sections can be swapped, another piece of better work from a classmate, and signed by the same issuer can be easily replaced. This is shown in diagrammatically in Fig. 2.10.

Furthermore, digitally signed documents are not editable after they are issued, not even by their issuer or owner; any modification will be detected. This is not suitable for the eCertificate as the owner would like to set controls on their distributed documents.

The system will employ a new signing method, the eCert signature, to ensure the integrity of the digitally signed eCertificate, so that the eCertificate can have the attached files securely bound together. Any unauthorized modification will be detected during the verification process, while it allows access control values to be changed while the certificate itself remains valid. This method will combine the detached signature and the enveloped signature, with condition statements to meet the specified eCertificate situation, as shown in the code below.

```
<metadata>
  <access time limit>,
  <transit_visible = 1>,
  <evidence_visible = 1>,
  .....
<qualification>
  <student ID>,
  < eCert ID >,
  <eCert time limit>,
  .....
  if <transcript_visible = 1> then validate the signature
              <transitfile>
                      < transcript_signaturevalue>
                      <Reference URI="...">
  if <evidence_visible = 1> then validate the signature
              <evidencefile>
                      < evidence_ signaturevalue>
                      <Reference URI="...">


  <qualification_signaturevalue>
```

Using this method, any changes to the signed content, either the qualification section, the transcript section, or the evidence section, will be detected; the owner-controlled access values can be changed in the metadata; the optional file will not be attached within an eCert file if it is set to 0 (representing nondisplay). This can minimize the transfer file size, while the signed document remains valid as the system will only carry on to verify and display the optional section if the condition in the metadata is met, such as the display value set to 1 (representing display). The file structure of an eCertificate is described diagrammatically in Fig. 2.11.

2.2.8.4 System Authentication and Verification

The management system is for students to view and/or set new access controls on their eCertificates. To ensure that only the owner can set controls on their own eCertificates but not other receivers, the management system will require a login control. This will consist of a combination match of the student ID and system password. The management system will verify the login student ID against the uploaded eCertificates.

The system will verify the embedded information in an eCert file every time it is accessed; failure of any single checking process will result in denial of access. These verification processes include:

- *Validate eCert access control time and date*
- *Validate eCert validation date*
- *Validate issuer's PKC against CRL*
- *Validate eCert status against eCert CRL*
- *Verify eCert ownership: eCert ID = login ID*
- *Verify content modification for the qualification section*

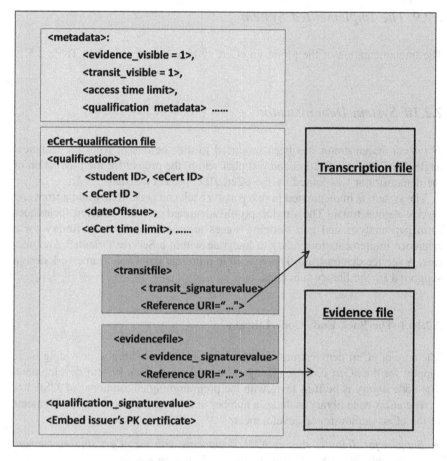

Fig. 2.11 eCertificate file structure design

- *Verify content modification for the transcript and/or evidence section(s), if the corresponding visible setting = 1.*

The actual interface of a valid eCertificate will contain the three files, as well as the verification result. The qualification award file will use a corresponding certificate image from the institution's system as background to maintain the look that a paper-based certificate has. It will contain the digital signature(s) of the signer(s). When the signature is clicked, the system will display a pop-up window with the information that the PKC can be traced all the way to the root CA.

2.2.9 The Implemented System

The implementation of the proposed eCert system is summarized in Table 2.5.

2.2.10 System Demonstrator

A system demonstrator has been produced to test the design from the technical angle. With the specification and test plan set up, the project for the production of the demonstrator was joined by the eCert JISC project assistant.

The system is implemented in two parts: a back end code library and a front end service demonstrator. The service profile identified and the selected techniques from gap analysis and gap bridging stages are used for the code library for a reference implementation, ready to integrate within a Service Oriented Architecture. A service demonstrator is produced to represent the whole framework design supported by the library functions.

2.2.10.1 The Back End: Code Library

The core of eCert demonstrator implementation is a code library, providing basic support for the eCert issuing, management, and verification system development. The code library is built in Java, with the programming environment of J2SE 1.6.

The eCert code library includes a number of features that meet the requirements of the eCert demonstrator development:

- *Support for digitally signing XML documents with the eCert signing method, compatible with ESTI European Digital Signature standard.*
- *Support for digitally signing and verifying files with given key stores.*
- *Support for Key Pair generating (variant lengths), converting (from/to String), and file encryption/decryption with RSA/DSA algorithm.*
- *Support for domain file processing, including producing qualification files, adding file metadata, setting access control, multiple digitally signing prepared files, file compression and decompression, and fully verifying signed qualification files.*

2.2.10.2 The Front End: Online Demonstrator

A web interface service demonstrator has been produced on top of the code library. The system is developed in MyEclipse Enterprise Workbench 8.5, and implemented using JSP, JavaScript (jQuery), and MySQL for the database.

Table 2.5 System implementation (SI)

DA ID	SI ID	Summary
DA-01	SI-01	The system was developed using XML to enable easy transition between systems with different platforms
DA-02	SI-02	The security control of hardware, database, and network for eCertificate generation and issuing processes is handled by the issuing institution
DA-03	SI-03	An in-built access control system is implemented
	SI-04	Based on their system role, only authorized staff can access the issuing system and only authorized students can access the management system, but everyone can access the verification system
DA-04	SI-05	Students can only set controls on their own eCertificates through the management system
	SI-06	Only reviewers with the correct access key can access the corresponding eCertificate
DA-05	SI-07	The traditional digital signing technique is used as the foundation of the signing process to support the content modification validation
DA-06	SI-08	Taking the signing key CRL as an example, a new qualification CRL has been created and its validation process added to the traditional digital signing process to solve the eCertificate squared problem
DA-07	SI-09	A function has been added to call for the verification of the signing key and display the result every time an eCertificate is accessed
DA-08	SI-10	A new file structure for eCertificate has been defined, which contains all elements that a paper-based certificate has, as well as the new elements the meet the eCertificate and ePortfolio requirements, such as the evidence file
DA-09	SI-11	The XML signature has been adopted with a new wrapping method for the various file types in the eCertificate to increase the signature security in the verification process
DA ID	SI ID	A timestamp has been added to the signature so that an eCertificate will be digitally signed, with certified signature time, thereby providing tamper evidence and nonrepudiation
DA-10	SI-12	Owner controlled access token, display sections, and access time limit values have been placed in metadata
DA-11	SI-13	A new signing method, eCert signature, has been implemented, which allows eCertificate owners to modify the metadata of a signed eCertificate without invalidating the signature
DA-12	SI-14	The system has been implemented with SOA
DA-13	SI-15	Standards and policies have been set up for all institutions which use the system

(continued)

Table 2.5 (continued)

DA ID	SI ID	Summary
	SI-16	As explained in the Unique Student ID and eCertificate ID section, a self-maintained numbering system has been implemented
DA-14	SI-17	An online center system has been implemented to provide eCertificate management and verification services. As the newly designed file structure and signing method enables the modification of access control values without re-signing, the system can be used independently from the issuers (with the last updated CRLs)
DA-15	SI-18	Support functions have been implemented to handle the complicated requirements from the back end, such signing and key management; therefore, front end web user friendly interface development can easily be set up by using the support functions
DA-16	SI-19	The system only provides the service, as no personal sensitive information is stored, it only stores the CRLs for validation purposes
DA-17	SI-20	As the implementation is based on traditional digital signatures, the PKI is maintained to provide trust between the stakeholders
DA-18	SI-21	The system was developed using XML to enable easy transition between systems with different platforms

The website provides the user interface for the issuing, management, and verification systems, with calls to the code library for functional support. All web pages share a common interface design for consistency with a different color scheme to distinguish the three systems. Different pages are rendered by loading different subpages in the menu and content areas using Ajax technologies.

2.2.11 eCert System Testing

Test preparation: 1. Create a Public key certificate for issuerA; 2. IssuerA issues an eCert, named eCertA, to userA through the issue system; 3. IssuerA issues an eCert, named eCertB, to userB through the issue system; 4. Create a user account for userA in the management subsystem.

The aim of this testing is, through the eCert demonstrator, to evaluate whether the proposed eCert system meets the requirements ID SR-03 and SR-04. After some debugging, the final test results were as expected. Details of the test plan and results are given in Table 2.6.

Table 2.6 eCert system test plan and result

SR ID	DT ID	Test items	Test method	Expect result	Test result
SR-03	DT-01	Unauthorized modification through displayed eCert	Access eCertA, change part of the displayed content, e.g., from BSc to PhD, and save as eCertD	The displayed content is read only. In case of being modified, it will not be a valid eCert	As expected: Can not modify the content of displayed eCert
	DT-02	Unauthorized modification through file code	Change the encrypted string for BSc to the one for PhD, save as eCertE (Assume a hacker can manage to access the qualification section of the eCert); then upload eCertE to the verification system	Displays error message (invalid digital signature)	As expected: returns a validation error without displaying eCert's content
	DT-03	Withdrawal of signer's key	Update the CRL for eCert issuers—revoke issuerA's key, then upload eCertA to the verification system	Display error message (key has been revoked)	As expected: Returns an error for validating issuer's PKC against CRL step in verification
	DT-04	Withdrawal of the qualification award	Update the CRL for eCert qualifications—revoke eCertB, then upload eCertB to the verification system	Display error message (award has been revoked)	As expected: Returns an error for CRL validation
	DT-05	Lifetime validation	Delete issuerA from the system; then upload eCertA to the verification system	Display the eCert	As expected: Displays the eCert

(continued)

Table 2.6 (continued)

SR ID	DT ID	Test items	Test method	Expect result	Test result
SR-04	DT-06	Unauthorized access	Open eCertA or eCertB with Microsoft Word, Notepad, IE, or XML editor (without any access key or system)	May achieve the encrypted string only, no meaningful data	As expected: Content of eCert files can not be accessed
			Login to the management subsystem as userA, upload eCertB with access token	Display error message (the user is not the owner of the uploaded eCert)	As expected: Returns an error for wrong user
			Access eCertA or eCertB through the verification subsystem without, or with incorrect, access token	Display error message (invalid access token)	As expected: Returns an error for wrong user
	DT-07	Authorized access	Login to the management subsystem as userA, upload eCertA with access token	Display the eCert	As expected: Verifies the eCert file and displays its content
			Access eCertA or eCertB with access token through the verification subsystem	Display the eCert	As expected: Verifies the eCert file and displays its content
	DT-08	User control of usage	Login to the management subsystem as userA, set new access token to eCertA, save as eCertC	Display the eCert when access is within the time limit; display error message when after the time limit	As expected: Verifies the eCert file and displays its content; Returns an error after the time limit expires without displaying the content of the eCert
			Access eCertC with access token through the verification subsystem within the time limit		
			Access eCertC again with access token through the verification subsystem after time limit		

2.2.12 Summary of Outcomes

A system has been developed following the SORM methodology. Based on the research decisions and assumptions for the new eCertificate system, a secure and user-centric approach has been presented to address the issues identified, such as the eCertificate squared problem and ownership rights. With a newly designed eCert file structure, signing method, and system structure, the new design enables authorized modifications to signed eCertificates while signature integration remains without the need of re-signing.

2.3 Evaluation Through ePortfolio Systems and the Delphi Method

The eCertificate is a new field of research, so at this starting point, the evaluation of the proposed system was focused on the theoretical level, such as whether the related issues have been understood and the design is appropriate, rather than on the production level of how well the demonstration system performs.

With this focus in mind, an experiment subproject, integrate eCert in ePortfolios, has been carried out to test the system against the requirement ID SR-01, evaluate whether the proposed eCert system can be adapted into the ePortfolio systems technically; Also, the Delphi methodology has been employed step-by-step alongside the eCert system development, to evaluate whether the proposed design meets all system requirements.

2.3.1 Evaluation Through Integrating eCert into ePortfolios

One of the goals of this eCertificate research is to investigate a solution for a secured eCertificate system that can overcome the paper-based certificate problems, and enable such eCertificates to be used standalone or serviced within other systems, most importantly the ePortfolio systems. The ePortfolios require verifiable qualification claims, and will be the main systems that the eCertificates are embedded in, therefore they are the best test-bed for the eCert system. A successful result of integrating eCertificates into ePortfolios will not only verify the applicability of the eCertificate system, but will also provide a solution for the ePortfolio artifacts' assertion issues. Therefore, after evaluating the eCertificate system through the Delphi method, the system is being evaluated again under a subproject named Integrating eCert in ePortfolios, to test its usage in the related applications.

2.3.1.1 The Selected ePortfolio Systems

Two ePortfolio systems were selected for the purpose of this study: eFolio[6] and Mahara.[7]

eFolio was selected as it is an in-house ePortfolio system. It was newly developed at the University of Southampton, which allows full access to both the code and the development team. The eFolio system is written in PHP and Java-Script, and allows authorized students to create a number of portfolios with their academic achievements. It is also used by staff for setting assignments and displaying coursework results. The system links with many central services provided by the University of Southampton, including the Banner student information system. The eFolio system was at its live-trial stage at the time of this research, and has not yet been released.

On the other hand, Mahara is mature and open source software, which has lots advantages over eFolio in terms of system functions and development environment. The Mahara system is written in PHP, and uses the Model-View-Controller (MVC) software architecture. The system's structure is highly modular; it contains several libraries to support its functionalities, has the capability of handling most of the eCert requirements, and offers a pluggable environment for customisation.

2.3.1.2 Systems Integration Analysis

The eCertificate file format: The structure of an eCertificate file is newly designed and developed, and contains three files: a qualification data file, a transcript file, and an evidence file. The main qualification file also holds the signatures for the related transcript and evidence files. All these are bound together, signed and encrypted, and named with a new file extension of .eCert. For the integration of eCert into an ePortfolio, the .eCert file must be able to be recognized and function as designed.

The eCert system: The eCert system includes two subsystems: the issuing subsystem for issuers to generate eCertificates; and the management and verification subsystem, an online service that enables users to upload their eCertificates. This allows owners to set access control to their eCertificates by adjusting particular variables, while reviewers can verify their received eCertificates. Assuming the eCertificate owners present their eCertificates by making them available as part of the ePortfolios, the ePortfolios have then become the user-friendly, web-based front-end, while the eCert Central System remains ultimately responsible for the management and verification process at the backend. For the integration of eCert

---

[6] eFolio: University of Southampton ePortfolio system. accessed on 2 March 2010; Available from: http://www.efolio.soton.ac.uk/

[7] Mahara: an open source ePortfolio system. accessed on 2 March 2010; Available from: http://mahara.org/

into ePortfolio, the eCert functions have to be maintained, so that eCertificates presented in ePortfolios are access controlled and verifiable.

2.3.1.3 The Challenge

The overall goal of this project was to integrate the eCert system into existing ePortfolio systems. From the system integration analysis above, it is clear that the challenge is to ensure the newly proposed eCertificate file, which has a unique file structure with file extension .eCert and secured by access key and digital signature, can be recognized and verified by the selected ePortfolio systems, eFolio and Mahara.

2.3.1.4 Development

With the ePortfolio systems selected and integration issues analyzed, a project specification was set up. The eCertificate integration development covered two segments: a new layer of Java code as the API for the eCert code library, and the extensions for eFolio and Mahara to enable the upload of eCertificates and their corresponding access keys, and the verification process with the eCert central services. Tests were carried out throughout the project to ensure that the system worked as expected and met the original requirements.

Full details of this eCertificate integration project can be found on the eCert project website.[8]

2.3.1.5 Results

From analysis and design to development and testing, the eCert in ePortfolio sub-project followed through the development lifecycle. As a result of successful implementation, both eFolio and Mahara can now be fully utilized by those with eCertificate qualifications. Thus we have proved that the newly developed eCertificate can be used in practice in real ePortfolio systems.

The project utilized the eCert code library. In the process, the eCert system was also been improved since errors were found and fixed.

---

[8] The eCert project (http://ecert.ecs.soton.ac.uk/): A JISC funded research project, aim to address the issues of design for a suitable user-centric "eCertificate" system.

2.3.2 Evaluation Through Delphi Methodology

The eCertificate study employed two research methodologies: SOAM and Delphi. The mini-Delphi methodology (Rowe and Wright 2001) was used step-by-step alongside the SORM methodology throughout the development stages, to guide and evaluate whether the design met all five requirements theoretically.

For the mini-Delphi method, a group of domain experts in the UK were selected for security system design, for ePortfolio analysis, and to represent the stakeholders. These included employment managers, IT security experts, exam board managers, and ePortfolio researchers. Two workshops were run during two stages of the development to collect professional opinions from these experts. The first one occurred at the system design stage, aiming to evaluate and adjust the design at the strategic level. After the first round of information collection, analysis, feedback, and system adjustment, a second workshop was run on the system demonstrator completion stage, when the system was shown to the domain experts again. The aim of this round was to evaluate and adjust the design not only at the theoretical level but also at the technical level.

2.3.2.1 The First Round of Delphi

Following the eCertificate research, analysis, and initial design phases, the first workshop was held to review the design before moving onto the demonstrator development stage. It took place in the International ePortfolio Development Centre at the University of Nottingham, and aimed to bring together leaders in the field to consider and report on design issues for the secure eCertificate system, to check whether the eCertificate problems and issues had been understood adequately, and that the project was on the right track for the solution.

The workshop was arranged in three parts: introduction to the eCertificate issues and problems through presentation; group discussions to explore and define the problem areas; and Round Table discussion on the proposed design and its related issues.

Following to the Delphi methodology, the first three phases (subject exploration, agreement analysis, and further exploration for disagreement) were carried out in this first round of evaluation: all conversations during group discussion were recorded and analyzed, disagreements and unaddressed issues were also explored. Full details of the feedback, analysis, and the actions taken are available from the eCert project website (Chen-Winson 2010). As a result, the system design was revised according to the workshop feedback.

2.3.2.2 The Second Round of Delphi

After system adjustment and further development, a second workshop was run. It was hoped that the variety of opinions would decrease and tend toward convergence.

The second eCert workshop was held at the end of the system demonstrator completion stage. The aim of the workshop was to evaluate the system design from the technical level, and work through the potential practical issues that might be encountered in the introduction of such a system. It took place during ALT-C2010, the 17th International Conference of the Association for Learning Technology, which was held at the University of Nottingham.

Following the Delphi method, the system was again presented to the domain experts. All participants from the first workshop had been invited to the second workshop, even though not everyone could make the second round, all new participants who joined the second workshop were experts in the domain.

During the workshop, the possibilities and potential problems of the eCertificate system were revisited. The questions were redesigned to reflect the topics that concerned the first workshop.

The first three phases of Delphi were carried out again in this second round evaluation: all conversations during group discussion were recorded and analyzed, disagreements and unaddressed issues also were explored. Full details are available on the eCert project website (Chen-Wilson 2010).

The feedback from this second workshop indicated that the eCert system would be of good use, and provide applications that would be enthusiastically welcomed. As a result, the system design was revisited according to the workshop feedback.

2.3.2.3 The Last Phase of Delphi

In addition to the two workshops with the domain experts, a few more workshops and presentations have also taken place at national and international computing security-related conferences to collect the opinions from a wider range of domain experts. These include: The 2nd International Conference on Computer Modelling and Simulation (ICCMS 2010), held in San Ya, China; The World Conference on Educational Multimedia, Hypermedia & Telecommunications (EdMedia 2010), held in Toronto, Canada; London Learning Forum, held in London, UK; Federated Access Management 2010 (FAM10), held at Cardiff, UK; and The World Congress on Internet Security (WorldCIS 2011), held in London, UK. The eCert system has thus been subject to continuous review and adjustment.

After each round, feedback was reflected upon and the system (including the design, demonstrator, documentation, and reports) adjusted accordingly. For example: the eCert file structure now includes the transcript file to enhance its usage nationwide; a photograph of the student can now be added as one of the evidence files and bound with the eCertificate to enhance the security, but optional when preferred for the sake of privacy; more work has been spent on comparing the new design and existing systems; and the explanation of the chosen approach has been given in more detail.

Toward the end of the project, much positive feedback was received from conferences and workshops internationally, while negative feedback was mainly related to the future work that cannot be completed within the current project.

As a result, this has proved that the eCertificate system can not only be used as a standalone application, but can also be plugged into other applications, such as ePortfolios. The eCert system's accessibility and scalability have also been improved after taking into account a considerable number of observations and recommendations from all the evaluation processes.

2.4 The Abstracted eCert Protocol and the Mobile eID Application

With the aim of proving that the eCert concept can be applied in a wider eDocument transmission domain, the eCert protocol was tested under a project, named Mobile eID, to explore the issues that arise in implementing the eCert protocol within a mobile platform to provide certified and verifiable identity information.

2.4.1 The Mobile eID Project

Technology development enables electronic identity (eID) to be employed in daily life, such as smart cards, online user accounts, and public key certificates. With the aim of replacing paper-based ID documents, these developments provide flexibility and efficiency with transportability.

Mobile devices have been constantly developed with a high computational complexity, providing flexible mobility, multi-functionality, and personal settings, and have become an indispensable daily object used more commonly than any other technical device, including the PC.

By combining eID development with the mobile environment, using the mobile device as the eID platform could realize the maximum benefit. In that case, all an individual's ID cards and documents can be left at home, and the mobile phone will be the only device needed.

However, combining these two also results in their problems being combined, which are of a wide variety but mainly about security. The challenges in this emerging area of technology adoption need to be considered and addressed.

2.4.1.1 Scenario

Consider the following situation: young-looking Bob often has to certify his age to purchase age-restricted products or get entry to clubs. By presenting his paper ID or ID cards, such as driving license, he is forced to disclose all the sensitive information on that document, such as address, not only the age. Unfortunately not all types of ID cards are acceptable in all situations, and he often left the required ID document at home. Disconsolate, Bob has to make a trip home.

The idea was to apply the eCert protocol to present ID documents as digitally signed, owner-controlled ID certificates through mobile devices.

2.4.1.2 Analysis

eID application development: an eID is an electronic document for online and offline identification, providing digitally the same (or more) information as the paper-based ID document, in many cases having more secure, flexible, and accessible functions. An eID is usually a plastic smart-card (or EIC), having printed identity information with an embedded microchip. The chip may also contain the issuer's signature keys and certificates. To use an EIC, the user will also need the card reader and the middleware software. Another form of eID is the public key certificate. As mentioned in earlier on the eCert system, a public key certificate is an eDocument which uses a digital signature to bind a public key with an identity, it is used to verify that a public key belongs to an individual.

eCertificate versus eID: The eCertificate and eID are both aimed at providing a secured and trusted system for the management of verified personal data. However, even though the eCertificate and eID are quite close in concept, their structures and execution environments are different.

- In a face-to-face situation, such as the clubbing scenario above, the eID system is a quick way of passing the eDocument to a reviewer for verification, rather than sending a request through email or accessing a website as the eCertificate system does.
- An eCert file is a collection of selectable support files, individually signed with references embedded in the main content, before it is signed and encrypted with the access control metadata. On the other hand, the ideal eID file will be a collection of selectable text information with an ID image gathered into a single signed file and encrypted together with the access control metadata. The eCert protocol needs to be adjusted to adapt the new eID file structure, so that it can be recognized by the verification process.
- The eCert protocol makes use of the eCertificate owner's institution account in the issuing process, which allows the eCertificate to be issued directly into the access controlled environment. In the eID, these accounts are unlikely to exist. Hence, a new encryption method to secure the issue process between the issuer and the eID owner is required.

- Unlike the eCertificate system, in which all issuers are under the umbrella of education institutions, and can have the issuers chased all the way back to the top education body, such as the UK Department for Education, the eIDs may be issued from a wide range of organizations. These could be driving license office, the General Register Office (GRO), or the Home Office. The eID system needs to be adjusted to suit this multiple top certification authority (CA) situation for the verification process.

2.4.1.3 Design

The aim of the Mobile eID system is to focus on the user-centric approach supported by the eCert protocol. Therefore, most of the eCert protocol features needed to be maintained. The initial eCert file structure needed to be adjusted, and the related functions needed to be modified to suit the eID's needs.

As anyone can potentially fake an eID on their own mobile phone, the process of verifying an eID needs to depend on the reviewers' devices. Therefore, even when an eID is presented face-to-face by its owner to the reviewer, a quick data transfer method is required to address the unique eID situation. After investigating current mobile communication techniques, such as email, Bluetooth, bar code, QR code,[9] and text messaging, the QR code with its increasing popularity and wide availability of a QR reader within mobile devices, proved to be the best solution for eID data transfer with its ability to transfer data quickly.

2.4.1.4 Development

Although the concepts of the eID and the eCertificate are quite close, they are different in many ways. The eCert protocol that was initially designed for managing eCertificates in a web environment is not able to manage eID in a mobile environment straight away—a reverse engineering process to adapt the system is needed (Zenise et al. 2011a).

The Mobile eID application has been implemented on the Android platform. The core of the application that employed the eCert methods was written in Java and linked to the Android interface with the use of PHP. The eCert file structure has been adjusted, the related functions have been modified to ensure that the new file structure could be maintained throughout the system, and a supporting function has been added to deal with the multiple top CAs situation, so that eIDs will remain valid as long as they can be tracked down to any of the top CAs. For example, on a successful eID validation, the system will display the name and photo, along with the selected information, within the time set by the owner. Figure 2.12 shows an eID displayed as QR code on mobile A. This is scanned and displayed on mobile B with a countdown of remaining display time.

---

[9] http://www.denso-wave.com/qrcode/index-e.html, accessed 22 Mar 2011.

Fig. 2.12   Verification of an eID

2.4.1.5   Evaluation

Through the Mobile eID project, problems relating to the employment of the eCert protocol in a mobile environment were identified and the eCert code library was adjusted accordingly. *Initial results indicate a real possibility of using the eCert protocol to manage eIDs in the mobile environment, supporting user-centric management of sensitive information* (Zenise et al. 2011b).

Besides the positive result obtained through system testing, a paper describing the protocol has also successfully passed the domain experts evaluation processes and has been published in the *International Journal for Infonomics*, (Zenise et al. 2011b).

As a result, the successful mobile eID application, which implemented a working demonstrator system on an Android platform, has proved that the eCert protocol can be applied in other eDocument transmitting domains.

However, the proposed system was only developed and tested "in house", no end users being involved. More issues need to be explored in this area in future study.

2.4.2   The Abstracted eCert Protocol

After being evaluated in two different applied domains, the eCert protocol has been improved to suit a wide range of file structures that may be required, for various types of user (including different ages, IT levels, and capabilities), and in various environments.

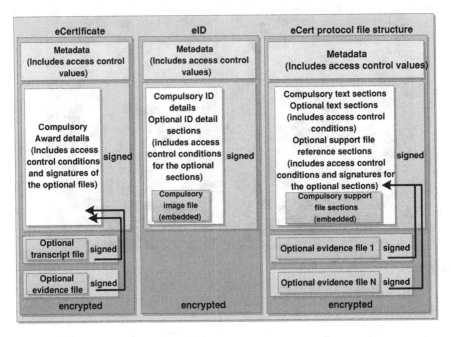

Fig. 2.13 eCert protocol file structure design

2.4.2.1 Features

File structure: an eCert file contains three types of data: metadata, text outputs, and file outputs (that can be in any format). These are constructed in three sections: metadata, main content, and detached supported files sections. Both the text content and the support files can be subdivided into two types: compulsory and optional. The text output forms the main content, whether compulsory or optional; the compulsory file outputs will be embedded within the main content, while the optional files will be attached. The improved file structure of the eCert protocol is shown in Fig. 2.13, along with the comparison of the earlier designs.

Signing method: optional files are signed individually using a detached signature. Their signature values and the reference URI are then embedded within the main content under the corresponding display conditions. The document is then signed using an enveloped signature, and encrypted before being distributed.

Key management: the system uses the issuer's private key to sign the document, and the system's default public key, or the receiver's public key to encrypt the document, depending on the applied situations or specified selected options. On review, the corresponding decrypt key, and the issuer's public key are used for verification.

System structure: all supported systems are installed locally in registered institutions, and link to the eCert central server. In addition, an online central service provides public access for the required management and verification service. In some cases, an identity management system is involved in access control.

Usage control: the owner can choose who can see what and for how long by setting usage control on section display and access time limits with a unique access token.

2.4.2.2 Advantages and Innovation

Secure: The eCert approach is based on digital signing, but also addresses what is called the "eCertificate squared" problem. Not only must the nonrepudiation and the authenticity of the document be ensured, but also the current validity covering the potential revocation of the data must be detected as the classical case of the revocation of the signing key. This means it is more secure than conventional digital signing.

User-centric: By taking this approach, ownership rights are addressed. The owner can not only store, manage, share, and track their personal data, but can also tailor their documents to best support their needs. In this way, the information is "under their control, with their consent, and for their benefit (Sadd 2010)."

Lifetime Validation: The eCert signing method and system structure design ensure that all issued eCert files are independent of the issuing body. They can therefore be validated for life even if the issuing body ceases to exist.

Verifiable Distributed Data: The eCert signing method also enables the distributed eDocument to be verified through a supported service, without the need for storing the data. This provides the advantage of saving huge storage and dramatically avoids database attacks.

2.4.3 Proof of Hypothesis

From this research, it has been shown that the hypothesis has been met. It has been described in Sect. 2.2 and has been tested and evaluated in Sects. 2.3 and 2.4:

1. Adapting the digital signature CRL method, maintaining the revocation lists for both the signer's key and the issued eCertificate, together with an automatic checking service against both of them. This not only solved the eCertificate squared issue but also improved the security of traditional digital signing with the verification process.
2. Employing a new file structure and a new signing method, allows the owner to set controls on the signed eCertificate through its metadata without invalidating the signature. This addressed the security issues of the new eCert system and satisfied the owner control requirement.

3. Applying 1 and 2, together with a new system structure design, and providing a central management and verification system independent from the issuing body, solved the lifelong nationwide availability usage issues.
4. The Mobile eID project has demonstrated that the eCertificate concept can be applied to a mobile environment.

From the designs, demonstrators, and approval processes that have taken place, the hypothesis has been proven not only at the theoretical level, but also in practice. The research outcome indicates that the improved eCert protocol can be applied successfully in a wide range of eDocument transmitting domains.

2.5 Conclusion

Arising out of initial interest in eCertificate research, a secure and user-centric eCertificate system has been proposed. It has successfully addressed the eCertificate squared problem that exists within the traditional digital signing method when it is applied to nonstatic content eDocuments. It has defined an eCertificate file structure, so that it contains not only the qualification award information, but also the transcript information and any supporting evidence files, which can be in any format. It has defined a new digital signing method to take into account the file structure and to meet the eDocuments' ownership rights. The new signing method not only binds the related files together, but also allows the eCertificate owners to set access control on the signed eDocument itself, specifying who can see what and for how. Meanwhile it retains the integrity of the signature, without the need for re-signing by the initial issuing body; an additional encryption key is added after the signing to ensure that only the receiver with the corresponding decryption key can access the file. The research has also proposed a newly designed centralized verification service for such digitally signed and access controlled distributed eCertificates. The system provides security control for verification against a specified eCertificate expiry time, access period, ownership, signing key status, qualification award status, and owner-controlled section display. The whole design works together to ensure the issued eCertificates can be securely distributed and verified independently from the issuing body and satisfy ownership rights, without requiring storage in the verification system. This method also provides the huge advantages of lifetime validation and the avoidance of many common database attacks.

The eCertificate system has been tested and evaluated through its demonstrator by following the selected research methodology. The design principle has been tested through a subproject, integrating eCert in ePortfolios, to evaluate the usage of eCertificates in other applications. The concept of the eCert solution has also been tested through a project, the Mobile eID, which evaluated the applicability of this concept in wider situations. It not only provided a valuable successful alternative test, but also an extremely interesting potential future application. The research has generated global interest from Australia to the USA and Canada. Current mobile technology puts limitations on what can be done, but it is immediately apparent to anyone using it that such an approach is simple to use and immensely powerful.

All the test and evaluation results were successful, indicating that the proposed eCert protocol will not only meet the eCertificate challenge, but it can also be applied to mobile eID, and applied to a wider eDocument transmission domain to solve security and controllability issues.

The main impact for eCert lies in the future. Now that the concept has been proven, and the protocol tested in differing contexts to ensure its broad applicability, the next step will be to roll out an eCert-based system and to test it with real users.

References

Abrami PC, Barrett H (2005) Directions for research and development on electronic portfolios. Can J Learn Technol 31(3):1–15

Chen-Wilson L (2010) The eCert project. 2010 [cited 2010; http://ecert.ecs.soton.ac.uk/]

CHESICC (2005) The certificate information verification services in China. http://www.chsi.com.cn/about_en/ Accessed 02 Sept 2008

Davis J (2009) Digital signatures application guidelines on digital signature practices for common criteria security, in MSDN Magazine

Digitary (2008) Secure electronic documents. http://www.digitary.net/aboutus.htm Accessed 12 Aug 2008

European Communities (2007) CERTIFICATE SUPPLEMENT: advanced certificate craft—electrical

European Communities (2008) InformationOn/EuropassCertificateSupplement/navigate.action. http://europass.cedefop.europa.eu/europass/home/vernav/Accessed 28 Jan 2008

Goldwasser S, Micali S, Rivest R (1988) A digital signature scheme secure against adaptive chosen-message attacks. SIAM J Comput 17(2):281–308

Hartnell-Young E et al (2006) Joining up the episodes of lifelong learning: a regional transition project. British J Educ Technol 37(6):853–866

Higgs P et al (2010) Trust federation user consultation and use-case collation, University of Southern Queensland's Link Affiliates

Kaliski B (2003) Raising the Standard for RSA Signatures: RSA-PSS (RSA Laboratories). http://www.rsa.com/rsalabs/node.asp?id=2005

Linstone HA, Turoff M (2002) The Delphi method: techniques and applications. Addison—Wesley, Reading, pp 618

Lysyanskaya A (2002) Signature schemes and applications to cryptographic protocol design, in electrical engineering and computer science. Massachusetts Institute of Technology (MIT), United States

Macnamara D, Drury C, Ward N (2010) Verifying VET learner attainment data—an investigation of learner verification services and third party verification needs, 2010, University of South Queensland Link Affiliates (Where is Report No or Journal or URL)

Macnamara D, Nicholas N, Miller A (2011) Accessing VET learner attainment data: an investigation to enable learner-facilitated electronic access to their VET learner attainment data. The Tertiary Education Research Database—education for work and beyond, 68

Mao W (2004) Modern cryptography: theory & practice. Prentice Hall, New Jersey, p. 308 (Professional Technical Reference)

Naedele M (2003) Standards for XML and Web services security. Computer 36(4):96–98

Network Working Group (2008) Internet X.509 Public Key Infrastructure Certificate and Certificate Revocation List (CRL) Profile, RFC5280

Papazoglou M (2003) Service-orientated computing: concepts, characteristics and directions. In: IEEE International Conference on web information systems engineering, Rome

Pfleeger CP, Pfleeger SL (2007) Security in computing, 4th edn. Prentice Hall, Englewood Cliffs

Pronichkin ARTEM OR DIMITRY? (2012) Certificate revocation list (CRL) verification—an application choice. 2012 12; Jan 2013; 29 Jul 2012: Available from: http://social.technet.microsoft.com/wiki/contents/articles/964.certificate-revocation-list-crl-verification-an-application-choice.aspx

Rivest R, Shamir A, Adleman L (1978) A method for obtaining digital signatures and public-key cryptosystems. Commun ACM 21(2):12–126

Rowe G, Wright G (2001) Expert opinions in forecasting: the Role of the Delphi technique. In: Armstrong J (ed) Principles of forecasting. Kluwer Academy Publishers, Norwellpp, pp 125–144

Royce P et al (2008) Report on on-line authentication of qualification records, 2008, MSc Computer Science Group Development Project, University of Southampton

Sadd G (2010) What do you think I am: trusted relationship management. In: London learning forum. London, UK

Saunders M, Lewis P, Thornhill A (2009) Research methods for business students, 5th edn. Pearson Education, Trans-Atlantic Publications Inc, UK

Selkirk A (2001) Using XML security mechanisms. BT Technol Jurnal 19(3):35–43

Sturcke J (2007) Government offers reward in hunt for lost data, in Guardian

W3C recommendation (2002) XML signature syntax and processing

Wills G et al (2006) FREMA: e-learning framework reference model for assessment. FREMA Project J. Available from http://www.frema.ecs.soton.ac.uk/projectJournal/

Zenise M, Vitaletti A, Argles D (2011a) A user-centric approach to eCertificate for electronic identities (eIDs) management in mobile environment. In: IEEE world congress on internet security (WorldCIS), 2011, London, UK

Zenise M et al (2011b) eIDeCert: a user-centric solution for mobile identification. Int J Infon 4(3/4):527–536

Zimmermann PR (1995) The official PGP user's guide. MIT Press, Cambridge